GARLAND STUDIES IN

THE HISTORY OF AMERICAN LABOR

edited by

STUART BRUCHEY
UNIVERSITY OF MAINE

A GARLAND SERIES

EMPLOYEE TURNOVER IN THE PUBLIC SECTOR

OSCAR MILLER, JR.

GARLAND PUBLISHING, INC.
NEW YORK & LONDON / 1996

331.126
M64e

Copyright © 1996 Oscar Miller, Jr.
All rights reserved

Library of Congress Cataloging-in-Publication Data

Miller, Oscar, 1958–
    Employee turnover in the public sector / Oscar Miller, Jr..
        p.   cm. — (Garland studies in the history of American
labor)
    Includes bibliographical references and index.
    ISBN 0-8153-2403-0 (alk. paper)
    1. Labor turnover—United States.   I. Title. II. Series.
HF5549.5.T8M557 1996
331.12'6'0973—dc20   95-52899

Printed on acid-free, 250-year-life paper
Manufactured in the United States of America

In memory of my mother, Phyllis J. Miller
(October 21, 1940 – December 31, 1976)

University Libraries
Carnegie Mellon University
Pittsburgh PA 15213-3890

Contents

Page

Tables

Preface

Studies of voluntary job exits show that quitting is determined by individual attributes, material compensation, and workers' affective response to work conditions. I argue that the authors of this research incorrectly assume that work conditions have an universal effect on all employees.

I use the locus of control personality construct to show how workers who believe that they can influence life events (internals) perceive and evaluation work conditions differently than workers who believe that life events are beyond their control (externals). I also develop a social exchange model of quitting which takes advantage of the positive (job reward) *and* negative (job cost) qualities inherent in work conditions. Workers tend to quit their jobs when job costs outweigh job rewards and when better alternatives exist. Moreover, personality interacts with employees' evaluation of job costs and rewards and quitting behavior.

The data with which to analyze quits comes from a census of 2846 social counselors, eligibility counselors, disability claims examiners, and vocational rehabilitation counselors employed by a state level government Human Services Agency (HSA) in June 1989. The social exchange model I develop is used in two analyses of quits. The first examines personality differences in perceiving and evaluating work conditions, and the interaction effect of personality and profit level on the odds of quitting. The second analysis examines the effect of occupation on perceptions and evaluations of work conditions and quitting. Finally, I test competing models of turnover to determine which best fits that data and is most generalizable.

Acknowledgments

I wish to thank my family and friends, especially my lovely wife, Tammy Kennedy-Miller. Thanks for all the love and moral support, thanks for everything.

Employee Turnover in the
Public Sector

I

Theory on Personality and Employee Turnover

There is perhaps no better way to examine human motivation than against the backdrop of the work setting. Karl Marx viewed work as the objectification of individuals; he believed that people are mirrored in the products of their labor and that these products reveal the maker to the outside world (Marx, 1977 [1867]). On a more practical note, the work process helps determine individuals' life chances, ideologies, values, and beliefs (see also Bourdieu, 1977a; Kohn, 1989). In market economies like that in the United States, one's occupation is a major determinant of personal and family lifestyle, psychological well-being and self and social identity (Gove and Gerkin, 1977). The institution of work is fundamental to life in the United States, and examining why workers quit their jobs is important to understanding basic human motivation. This book addresses human motivation by examining quitting behavior to understand why some employees leave work situations that many believe are basic to lifestyle, psychological well-being, and self and social identity when others stay in these same jobs.

Current explanations of quitting behavior derive primarily from structural and psychological theory on human behavior. Structural theory posits that complex social institutions like governments, economies and organizations pattern behavior through hierarchial authority relationships, job descriptions, rules and regulations, incentives and disincentives. These structures (ie., work conditions) both constrain and enable the actions of employees (Ritzer, 1989). Quitting and staying are responses to these constraining and enabling work conditions (Price, 1977). Psychological theory argues that internal processes like drives (Freud, 1962; Hall and

Lindzey, 1970), behavioral propensities (Smith, 1965[1776]), and attitudes and values (Allport, 1967; Fishbein, 1967b) determine when employees are likely to quit their jobs.

Elements of structural and psychological theory have been combined to model quitting behavior (Mobley et al, 1979). Other influential work on turnover ignores psychological variables like personality (Price, 1977). No research takes full advantage of the mounting evidence uncovered in studies that simultaneously examine both structural and psychological variables to explain the determinants of quitting. One possible reason for this oversight may be that no theory has been identified that adequately bridges the gap between individual and institutional level theories of quitting behavior.

Kohn (1981, 1989) and Moos (1986) posit theory concerning individual behavior and attitudes in work settings and how these relate to social structure. Kohn argues that the relationship between work conditions and personality is reciprocal. Moos suggests that personality determines how employees perceive work conditions. Neither Kohn nor Moos specifies the relationship between personality, work conditions, and turnover. Some writers argue that recent sociological research tends to focus on the role of social structure while losing sight of individual agency (Cornfield, 1987; Kalleberg, 1989; Ritzer, 1989; Simpson, 1989). Nowhere is this neglect more apparent than in the study of employee quitting behavior. Current economic, psychological, and sociological theory on quitting behavior either ignores or misspecifies the role that personality plays in defining the work environment and determining workplace behavior.

Using a social exchange theory—a model of human action that views social relationships as bonds that form between rational actors as they exchange material, social, and psychological resources—I argue that personality influences how employees perceive resources exchanged in the workplace, and the relative value of these resources. Moreover, termination of the bond between employees and employers (i.e.,quitting behavior or turnover) is determined in the context of exchanges between employees, who provide labor and skills, and employers, who provide material and social resources. Turnover is regulated by personality, the type and value of exchange resources, and the interaction between personality and exchange resources. I examine this assumption by: 1) reviewing economic, sociological, and psychological theory on employee turnover, 2) developing a social exchange theory of quitting behavior, and 3) developing and testing specific hypotheses about the relationship among personality, work conditions, and turnover. After accomplishing these three tasks, I discuss the relevance of my findings for current and future research.

THEORIES OF TURNOVER

Proponents of economic, psychological, and sociological models of turnover have contributed to a growing body of evidence on quitting behavior. Most of this research is distinguished by a tendency among investigators to explore turnover from within a single disciplinary framework. To highlight the determinants of turnover that have been identified by researchers in these disciplines, the following review of literature is organized into sections on economic, psychological, and sociological theory.

Contributions from Economics

Economic models of employee turnover derive from utility maximization, dual labor market, and human capital theories. These theories posit that principles of supply and demand drive behavior; they differ in the extent to which supply and demand principles apply to individuals or larger market forces.

Utility maximization (UM) models of employee turnover view workers as rational actors who pursue profit in the labor market. Employees tend to react to the economic conditions of employment rather than creating the conditions of their employment. Since employees seek to maximize earnings and benefits, variation in compensation between different employment relationships helps to explain turnover (Armknecht and Early, 1972; Utgoff, 1983). Ippolito's (1987) UM model shows that pension structures affect turnover rates across market sectors. He argues that pensions comprise a greater portion of total compensation for federal employees than for municipal and private sector employees; federal employees who quit their jobs forsake substantial accrued benefits. Therefore, turnover rates are generally lower in federal jobs than in municipal and private sector jobs. Utility maximization models show that employees leave lower paying jobs when they have the opportunity to make more money elsewhere. The view that employees are rational actors who are constrained and enabled by economic forces finds support in evidence that shows that, over time, aggregate quit rates covary with the business cycle (Price, 1977:81-84). That is, during economic expansion, when jobs are plentiful, employees can bargain for better compensation packages and turnover rates increase. During economic contractions, employers have the bargaining edge; jobs are harder to find and turnover rates decrease. Alternative economic models of employee turnover are required to explain who quits and who stays in jobs under similar economic conditions.

Dual labor market (DLM) theory argues that the economy is segmented into primary and secondary labor markets which are distinguished by different work environments (c.f., Averitt, 1968). The primary market provides employees with high wages, good work conditions, stable employment, job security, and equity in due process in the administration of work rules and chances for advancement. Opposite conditions exist in the secondary labor market (Piore, 1972). DLM theorists have successfully explained how labor market segmentation affects work outcomes such as gender and race income differentials (Howell and Reese, 1986), industry wage differentials (Krueger and Summer, 1987), employee loyalty (Doeringer and Piore, 1971), and quit rates (Armknecht and Early, 1972; Cornfield, 1985).

Employees generally find conditions in the primary sector more satisfying (Braverman, 1974; Hodson and Sullivan, 1985). Primary sector organizations offer internal labor markets, a series of job ladders that give employees opportunities to move vertically and horizontally within the organization (Diprete, 1987). Employees who have these options leave organizational boundaries less often than employees who have no such opportunities (March and Simon, 1958; Todor and Dalton, 1986). These findings suggest that work conditions other than pay and compensation affect employee quitting decisions.

Dual labor market models of employee turnover primarily consider how compensation packages affect employee turnover in various labor markets. The size of organizations, their products or services, government versus private ownership, pay scales, and benefit packages identify several labor markets. Turnover studies in the DLM tradition show that employees in jobs with poor work conditions and low wages, which characterize secondary labor market firms, tend to have higher voluntary quit rates than employees in primary sector firms (Hodson and Sullivan, 1985). Research shows that pay rates for identical jobs vary across sectors (Perloff 1971; Utgoff, 1983; Ippolito, 1987; Leonard, 1987), and that industry wage differentials persist over time (c.f., Krueger and Summer, 1987).

Perloff (1971) found that municipal salaries are higher than federal salaries, and that municipalities and federal governments tend to pay more than private industry, for the jobs he considers. Overall, quit rates are lower in the government sector than in the private sector (Utgoff, 1983). Perloff's (1971) and Utgoff's (1983) findings that lower rates of turnover occur among government employees, when compared with private sector employees, support the general premise of DLM models of employee turnover. That is, government jobs have better work conditions and experience lower turnover. DLM models of employee turnover also find support from research showing that pension plans affect turnover rates among federal employees, when compared with private sector employees (Ippolito, 1987).

Dual labor models of turnover are limited in that they focus on factors that affect aggregate turnover rates. These models find the causes of turnover within the structure of organizations or industries, but reveal little about how employee attributes or job characteristics common to firms across sectors affect employees' decisions to leave organizations or transfer within organizations. DLM models also offer no explanation for the timing of turnover among individuals, nor do they provide a good description of the types of employees who are at greater risk of quitting (Mobley, 1982).

The final economic model of employee turnover that I examine derives from human capital theory (c.f., Becker, 1975). Human capital (HC) theory posits that individual attributes determine individuals' initial placement in the workplace and subsequent quitting behavior. Human capital refers to employees' skills, education, and training. Employees exchange human capital with employers for pay, benefits and work conditions. Proponents of this theory argue that individual differences in the amount of human capital employees possess determine their opportunities in the marketplace. Employees who have more human capital should be more capable, and likely, to move into better employment relationships than employees who have less human capital (Becker, 1975).

Some research supports HC models of employee turnover (Greenhalgh, 1980; Distefano and Pryer, 1982). Greenhalgh considers the turnover process in terms of five stages in employees' careers. He argues that highly skilled employees have more job opportunities than employees who have more generic skills, and are more likely to turn over at each stage. Greenhalgh also found that highly skilled employees examine job conditions more carefully during the recruitment stage. In contrast, Distefano and Pryer (1982) observe no significant differences between stayers and leavers on human capital variables such as education, prior work experience, ability, and training performance tests. These disparate findings can, however, be reconciled within HC theory.

Employees who have a lot of human capital also tend to have more invested in their jobs and are more specialized than employees who have less human capital. Specialized skills are less transferable than general skills

(Becker, 1975), and employees who invest heavily in their jobs tend to remain in them (Farrell and Rusbutt, 1981). These competing forces identify a weakness in human capital explanations of turnover. Since highly trained and specialized employees own valued skills that are often non-transferrable, HC variables can have a positive or a negative influence on turnover. Determining the strength and direction of these relationships is difficult. Assessing the net effect of having specialized skills versus portable training on turnover, and identifying which attribute has the larger impact are empirical questions that require further study.

Utility maximization, dual labor market, and human capital models of turnover show that healthy and poor economic conditions, economic structures, and the human capital owned by employees affect employee turnover. Research that examines variation in these economic characteristics shows that wage differentials and compensation packages are the primary determinants of employee turnover; net of other effects, employees who receive higher wages are less likely to quit than employees who receive lower wages. However, employees can only take advantage of better compensation outcomes when opportunities exist (March and Simon, 1958; Armknecht and Early, 1972; Greenhalgh, 1980). The fundamental contribution that economic models make to the turnover literature is in identifying how economic conditions distribute opportunity among employees. Employees with more opportunities are more mobile. In the primary labor market, internal labor markets and human capital variables determine mobility opportunities. Opportunity in the secondary labor market depends on generic and low skill requirements and the availability of low paying, low reward jobs.

Economic models do not explicitly address issues of individual agency in perceiving, creating, and capitalizing on employment opportunities. Research shows that some employees can change jobs even under depressed economic conditions (Granovetter, 1973), suggesting that non-economic factors such as the opportunity that derives from personal contacts may affect quitting decisions (Wegener, 1991). Recent debate on the effect of objective versus subjective measures of employment opportunity on turnover supports this assertion (March and Simon, 1958; Muchinsky and Morrow, 1980; Hui, 1988). This debate highlights the significance of individual contacts, market awareness, and opportunity in predicting turnover.

Future research must provide clearer insight into the problem of why some employees quit their jobs while others, under similar working and economic conditions, do not. Explanations of this kind require knowledge of employee personalities and their perceptions about work and the work environment (c.f., Buss and Craik, 1985; Colavelli and Dean, 1987; Gerhart, 1987). That is, personality interacts with objective measures of employee compensation and other work conditions to determine how individuals perceive opportunity. The following section examines theories and models of turnover that consider how work values and attitudes affect turnover.

Contributions from Psychology

Proponents of psychological models of turnover argue that individuals attribute positive and negative qualities to work conditions. Affective responses to objects determine behavior toward those objects (cf., Fishbein, 1976b; Hill, 1981). The process of attitude and value formation is the subject of research that examines how learning occurs (Berger and Lambert, 1968; Hall and Lindzey, 1970; Shaw and Costanzo, 1970). Understanding how individuals learn is pertinent to studies of quitting behavior because learning encompasses the processes of attitude and value formulation, which many regard as antecedents of behavior (c.f., Fishbein, 1967b; Hill, 1981). Many psychologists argue that individuals learn attitudes and behaviors according to principles of reinforcement described in learning theory (Berger and Lambert, 1968; Hall and Lindzey, 1970; Shaw and Costanzo, 1970).

In turnover research, reinforcements are work conditions that strengthen or diminish the odds that employees will remain in their jobs. Turnover results from individuals' positive and negative evaluations of workplace reinforcers. According to proponents of learning theory, reinforcers can be material and nonmaterial, economic and social. Employees may perceive earning an income, fringe benefits, or favorable performance evaluations as positive economic reinforcements. Conversely, employees may perceive pink slips, pay reductions, and disapproving evaluations as negative reinforcements. Work conditions like required travel or employer expectations of overtime may be enjoyed by some employees and disliked by others.

Social reinforcements may include expressions of social approval and disapproval for job performance (e.g., from supervisors, co-workers and clients) and the social prestige afforded occupations. It is important to reemphasize that the positive or negative reinforcement qualities that employees attach to work conditions is an empirical question; it is misleading to suggest that the same work conditions reinforce all individuals uniformly. Behaviors that elicit positive responses tend to continue (Berger and Lambert, 1968; Shaw and Costanzo, 1970). Employees who perceive more positive than negative reinforcements from their jobs are less likely to quit than are employees who perceive more negative than positive reinforcements. The learning theory of turnover suggests that organizations that offer "better" reinforcements (or work conditions) are likely to experience lower rates of turnover.

Principles of learning theory are evident in many studies of employee turnover. Most of this research examines the effects of employee commitment to organizations (i.e., employee loyalty to organizations, attachment to organizational goals) and satisfaction with organizations and jobs on turnover (c.f., Mobley, 1982; Mowday, Steers, and Porter, 1979; Mowday et al,. 1982). Other research examines the relationship between behavioral intentions (employees' stated belief about future behavior) and employee turnover (c.f., Spector and Michaels, 1986). Satisfaction and commitment models evidence traces of learning theory, especially in terms of how people learn attitudes.

The formulation of work attitudes is consistent with principles of learning theory (Doob, 1967; Rhine, 1967; Rosenberg, 1967; Smith, 1967; Staats, 1967a; Staats and Staats, 1967; Lott and Lott, 1985). One concern of many researchers in this area is the relationship between attitudes and behavior. Although evidence of the exact nature of this relationship is inconclusive, research generally indicates that attitudes affect behavior, and that behavior modifies attitudes (Chein, 1967; Doob, 1967; Fishbein, 1967b; LaPiere, 1967; Lott, 1967; Staats and Staats, 1967).

Two categories of turnover models are grounded in attitude theories. The first describes quitting behavior in terms of strategy that individuals use to manage stressful situations. This model views employee turnover as an adaptive response to stress arising from conflict between work attitudes and work conditions. Typically, this model describes how characteristics of organizations produce stress in employees and how employees deal with stress by quitting or remaining in their jobs. Proponents of this "coping" theory of turnover assume that jobs that contain few stressors are more satisfying to employees (see Mobley et al. [1979] for a review of this literature).

Research that finds a significant correlation between positive aspects of jobs and job satisfaction, and a similar relationship between satisfaction and turnover, provides support for "satisfaction" models of turnover (Koch and Steers, 1978; Mobley et al., 1979; Rusbult and Farrell, 1983). However, the magnitude of the correlation between satisfaction and turnover is generally low (Locke, 1976; Waters, Roach, and Waters, 1976; Mobley et al., 1979). Related work considers how the level of commitment that employees have to their job affects turnover (Koch and Steers, 1978; Mobley et al., 1979; Price and Mueller, 1981; Mowday, Porter, and Steers, 1982; O'Reilly and Chatman, 1986), with similarly weak correlations.

A second model that describes the relationship between attitudes and turnover examines how behavioral intentions affect turnover. This model provides the best predictions of turnover (Mobley, 1982; Michaels and Spector, 1986; Weisberg and Kirschenbaum, 1993). An employee's intention to quit develops with other attitudes about life, job, and work behavior. This "cognitive structure" is the best predictor of employees' behavior (Fishbein and Ajzen, 1975:369). Recently, many studies of employee turnover have examined the effect of behavioral intentions on employee turnover (for a recent review article see Carsten and Spector, 1987).

Behavioral intentions are individuals' expressed expectations to engage in specific behaviors. Research indicates that employee turnover intentions are significantly correlated with turnover (Youngblood, Mobley, and Meglino, 1983; Steel and Ovalle, 1984). However, intentions change systematically over time (Youngblood et al., 1983). Others argue that attitudes and behavior are remarkably stable over time (Buss and Craik, 1985; Staw, Bell, Clausen, 1986). The apparent inconsistency in these findings disappears upon consideration that individuals realign dissonant attitudes to be more consistent with their cognitive structure, which remains relatively stable over time (Totman, 1973).

Although research on the relationship between behavioral intentions and turnover generally supports the argument that behavioral intentions are the best predictors of behavior, the results are substantively weak. The findings add little to our understanding of which characteristics of jobs or employees determine quitting behavior. Other research examines the relationship between job characteristics and turnover in much the same way.

Research that considers how dispositions influence behavior helps to explain which attitudes are likely to have the greater impact on behavior. Proponents of dispositional models maintain that individuals are predisposed to certain attitudes, and that these personality traits are more important for predicting behavior than are characteristics of jobs (Staw and Ross, 1985; Staw, Bell, and Clausen, 1986). One disposition that receives a lot of attention in turnover research is the Locus of Control (LOC) construct. LOC refers to an individual's tendency to perceive that behavioral reinforcements derive from either external or internal sources, or from luck or personal agency. Individuals' expectations about the source of reinforcements accumulate from events that occur over a lifetime (Lefcourt, 1982:1-18; Ganster and Fusilier, 1989). Rotter (1966) argues that knowledge of these expectations, personal values, and situational factors can aid in predicting action. LOC also structures individual perceptions about objects and events and helps shape attitudes about objects and events (Staw et al., 1986).

Individuals who have an external LOC (externals) are less goal-oriented than people who have an internal LOC (internals). Externals do not cope as well with stressful situations as do internals, and should quit stressful jobs more than employees who have an internal LOC (Andrisani and Nestel, 1976; O'Brien, 1984). In fact, however, the evidence shows no significant difference in turnover between internals and externals (Spector and Michaels, 1986). This suggests that "disposition" models that overlook other important characteristics of individuals and jobs are inadequate for explaining employee turnover.

LOC theory neglects the role that opportunity and resource value play in determining favorableness of turnover options for internals and externals. LOC has no direct effect on quitting but theory suggests that direct and indirect effects should exist. Internals may quit more than externals when work goals are not met. Internals show a greater focus on achieving goals—this may obscure their view of negative work situations, and make the workplace a less stressful and costly environment for them than it is for externals. Therefore, LOC would have indirect effects on quitting decisions. To resolve this issue, positive and negative job reinforcers should be measured as characteristics of jobs that do and do not support the psychological requirements of internals and externals.

Contributions from Sociology

Sociological theory on employee turnover examines the effect of the work situation on quitting behavior. In doing so, situational models counter the individual reductionism implicit in disposition models, unfortunately, with their own brand of reductionism. This approach argues that job or organizational characteristics are better predictors of job satisfaction and commitment than individual factors (Price, 1977; Koch and Steers, 1978; Glisson and Durick, 1988; Kohn, 1981, 1989; Graham and Keeley, 1992;

Mueller, Wallace, and Price, 1992; Saunders, Shepard, Knight, and Roth, 1992; Agho, Mueller, and Price, 1993 Mueller, Boyer, and Price, 1994). The study of the relationship between situational variables and turnover is where psychology and sociology merge. Kohn (1981, 1989) shows that complex work conditions promote higher intellectual functioning, and that employees who score higher on intellectual functioning create dynamic and challenging work environments. This evidence suggests that various set of work conditions may be a better fit for employees with corresponding personality traits. However, the primary thrust of Kohn's work is toward identifying how individuals create social structures and how social structures affect individual development rather than the role personality plays in perceiving and evaluating social structures (i.e. work conditions).

Price's (1977) oft-cited model describes the relationship between several characteristics of jobs, satisfaction, opportunity, and turnover. This model is the classic sociological explanation of turnover. It is argued that some situational variables constrain while others facilitate action, and they increase or decrease the absolute level of employee satisfaction. Price shows that satisfaction is negatively associated with turnover, while the level of economic opportunity moderates this relationship. Later efforts show that the interaction between opportunity and satisfaction is not significant, and that opportunity is an antecedent to job satisfaction (Bluedorn, 1982).

Price (1977), Halaby and Weakliem (1989), and much of the psychological research on turnover underscore the importance of analyzing how employees and work conditions interact to shape work attitudes, and as I argue, quitting behavior. However, this literature considers only how personality directly interacts with work attitudes such as job satisfaction and commitment to determine turnover. The idea that employees will have different attitudes about the same work conditions is absent in the turnover literature. In fact, Moos' (1986) social ecological theory is one of the few to address the work domain x personality interaction. Although Moos does not devote much space to articulating his ideas about this relationship, the model he presents has heuristic value. Moos' model posits a link between organizational and work factors, non-work factors (e.g., family and neighborhood stressors), occupation, socio-demographic characteristics, personal resources (e.g., self-esteem, intellectual ability), cognitive appraisals, coping responses, health and well-being, and work morale and performance. Moos (1986:12) explains the link between personality and the work domain as follows:

Cognitive appraisal is the outcome of an interplay between the personal and environmental systems. Consider a work group in which employees determine the allocation and sequence of specific tasks, the timing of rest breaks, and the principles underlying variations in pay. Most observers are likely to appraise such a group as high on involvement and autonomy, but an individual who is oriented toward external control (personal system) might see it as chaotic and disorganized.

Moos' model, however, links variables without identifying the content of the relationship between variables in a way that suggest any clear hypotheses. Such a vague framework is not suited to predicting quitting behavior. I argue that more insight into the person x work domain interaction, and its effect on quitting behavior, is obtainable using a social exchange approach that extends past research by specifying relationships between personality (i.e., dispositions) and situational variables (i.e., work conditions).

Debate between disposition and "situation" perspectives on employee turnover has produced many studies, but neither perspective has garnered conclusive empirical support (Snyder and Ickes, 1985). An obvious resolution to this debate would be to synthesize elements in the two views that have produced strong evidence on the determinants of turnover. Recent research does show the need for such a synthesis. Studies of interaction effects show that opportunity (Carsten and Spector, 1987), behavioral intentions (Youngblood, Mobley, and Meglino, 1983; Steel and Ovalle, 1984), performance, (Orpen, 1986), tenure (Werbel and Gould, 1984), and personality variables moderate the relationship between satisfaction and turnover, and between commitment and turnover (Sims, Szilagyi, and Keller, 1976; Archer, 1979; Mobley et al, 1979; Tziner, 1984; Werbel and Gould, 1984; O'Reilly and Chatman, 1986; Spector and Michaels, 1986; Krecker, 1994).

The studies discussed above illustrate an "interaction" approach that uses concrete criteria such as opportunity, performance, and tenure, or personality criteria as moderators. Studies also show that locus of control (Rotter, 1966; Spector and Michaels, 1986), definition of the situation (Goffman, 1959), anxiety (Endler and Magnusson, 1976), and delayed gratification (Griffeth and Hom, 1988) moderate the relationship between situational factors and behavior, and the process of attitude change (Phares, 1973, Singer, 1981). Some of this research helps to explain the relationship between satisfaction and turnover.

Other research that shows how personality interacts with situational factors aids in identifying the predictors and determinants of satisfaction. Determinants of satisfaction include factors like the fit between worker and organizational values (Gottfredson, 1978; Wiggings, Lederer, Salkowe, and Rys, 1983; Furnham and Schaeffer, 1984; Farris, Youngblood, and Yates, 1985). Predictors of satisfaction include role ambiguity (Abdel-Halim, 1981; Beddian and Armenakis, 1981) and skill variation or complexity (Katz, 1978; Dewar and Werbel, 1979; Haynes, 1979; Abdel-Halim, 1981; Gerhart, 1987). However, Mowday and Spencer (1981) observe no interaction between personality, situational variables, and turnover.

Economic, Psychological, and Sociological Theory

In summary, psychological perspectives on employee turnover suggest that knowledge of work attitudes and values improves prediction of employee turnover over that of economic theories. Attitude research seeks to understand the relationship between attitudes and behavior. Models of employee turnover that are based on attitude research differ from economic models in that they suggest that employees possess attributes that go beyond those reflected in the narrow view of employees as rational economic actors. Employees possess attitudes that predispose them to perceive work conditions in ways that determine the odds that they will change or remain in their jobs.

The sociological literature on employee turnover is sparse compared to research based on economic and psychological perspectives. Sociological and situational models offer important information about job characteristics that employees may find distressing, and therefore, that tend to promote turnover. Research shows that situational models are most appropriate for predicting satisfaction, while disposition models best predict commitment (Koch and Steers, 1978; Colarelli, Dean, and Konstans, 1987; Glisson and Durick, 1988). The primary difference between economic, psychological, and sociological theory on organizational behavior appears to be the nature of the question that each theory of turnover addresses.

Judging from the explanatory variables employed in sociological models of turnover, the sociological question seems to be concerned with understanding if the bureaucratization of work constrains individual initiative and creativity to the point where individuals seek more autonomy and control in their lives by leaving restrictive work situations. The question that proponents of psychological models of turnover appear to ask is which job characteristics are most stressful, and how personality affects individual coping behavior. Economic models seem to be concerned with how economic conditions, organizational characteristics, and employee skills and training affect their opportunities to maximize profit in the labor market. The assumption is that rational economic actors will seek to take advantage of available opportunity.

Economic, psychological, and sociological questions are distinct, but the answers require conceptual and methodological overlap across the disciplines. This is evidenced by integrative models of employee turnover from each perspective that are among the most cited research of this kind (March and Simon, 1958; Price, 1977; Mobley et. al., 1979). All of the assumptions that economists, psychologists, and sociologists make about the factors that determine variation in turnover can be accommodated in a refined theory of exchange behavior presented in the following section.

Predicting turnover and the termination of other exchange relationships requires an understanding of attitudes and values, and their relationship to behavior. All human interaction involves exchange of some kind (Blau, 1964; Homans, 1974). Individuals interact with a variety of social actors that may include private and public actors (e.g., individuals, nations, corporations). Characteristics of each of these actors, and the cultural and physical settings in which interaction occurs, affect exchanges. The economic, psychological, and sociological models discussed above provide inadequate explanations of human motivation and behavior and, specifically, quitting behavior. Successful explanation of human action requires consideration of strengths in each perspective. As they are used in turnover research, each model implies that principles of reinforcement are operative in quitting behavior.

Economic, psychological, and sociological research that finds that employee satisfaction, commitment, structural variables, and pay rates affect employee turnover supports the role of reinforcement theory in determining turnover. The unifying theme in these theories is that quitting behavior is an employee's reaction to work conditions and economic conditions. However, previous research does not consider that not all workplace phenomena hold universal meaning and that some workplace phenomena may only have meaning in specific contexts. Imputing universal meaning to workplace phenomena simplifies the contextual arrangement of behaviors, which leads to an inaccurate picture of individual behavioral antecedents. As conceptual tools, reinforcement and profit maximization are too ambiguous to specify all the resources and experiences exchanged in the workplace that individuals find rewarding.

Social Exchange Theory

Social exchange theory asserts that individuals build relationships by trading resources they own for those they need or want through formal and informal transactions. Transactions involve exchanges of material (e.g., wages, promotions) and social resources (e.g., approval, praise). Proponents of social exchange theory argue that these exchanges provide the materials and social interaction necessary for individuals to survive, including the fundamental process of organizing isolated individuals into cohesive populations (c.f., Smith, 1965(1776); Emerson, 1981). As such, exchange theory is useful for explaining behavior in romantic relationships (Rusbult, 1980), interdependent relationships (Thibaut and Kelly, 1959; Blau, 1964), service provider-client relationships (Emerson, 1962; Molm, 1989), and professions and organizations (Schoenherr and Greeley, 1974:407; Farrell and Rusbult, 1981; Rusbult and Farrell, 1983; Eisenberger and Huntington, 1986; Verdieck, Shields, and Hoge, 1986; Blegen and Lawler, 1989; Farrell and Rusbult, 1992). Since employment is the exchange of effort and loyalty for material or social rewards (March and Simons, 1958; Mowday, Porter, and Steers, 1982), exchange theory should prove equally beneficial in explaining why employees quit or remain in their jobs.

Writers make several core assumptions about exchanges (Blau, 1964:1-82; Emerson, 1972, 1981; Heath, 1976:1-74; Homans, 1974:1-82). First, actors participating in exchanges make rational decisions regarding the content of transactions; and transactions do not occur, or exchange relationships tend to be terminated, if actors do not receive expected benefits (Blau, 1964:6; Homans, 1974). Second, reinforcements are subject to principles of diminishing marginal utility, satiation, or value adaptation (Emerson, 1981:32). Third, the benefits one receives through social interaction depend on the benefits one provides in exchange. Fourth, mutually beneficial transactions can produce long-term exchange relations (Blau, 1964). Trust, non-contractual obligations and commitment among exchange partners develop over time between persons in exchange relationships.

The assumptions of social exchange theory directly address individual-level factors that contribute to quitting behavior and can explain why and how previously identified determinants of turnover relate to quitting behavior. Moreover, employing a social exchange approach to study quitting behavior facilitates explanation of the person × work-domain interaction. This interaction can be expressed in terms of the value of commodities in person-workplace transactions. Therefore, one way to understand the person-work interaction is to determine how employees value work conditions.

Until recently, social exchange theory offered no clear statement of what determines the value of commodities that exchange partners trade. Without knowing how the respective exchange partners value commodities, it is impossible to calculate accurately the costs, rewards, or the overall profit associated with transactions. Emerson (1981) suggests that need, uncertainty, and the reinforcing nature of objects determine how much value they hold. Need refers to the biological requirement organisms have for inputs such as oxygen, water, and food. According to Emerson, the need attached to a given input is an objective measure of value that is assessed by ranking it with less urgent inputs. Uncertainty refers to the ambiguity surrounding the benefits of a given need. If a need has an uncertain benefit, that input is usually highly valued. These assumptions lead Emerson to argue that the high degree of uncertainty surrounding the results of medical practices accounts for their high cost. Finally, objects that are conditioned or generalized reinforcers have more value because they are associated with past primary sources of benefit. Therefore, people value money more than other resources such as bacon, cheese, or bread because experience teaches them that money can be converted into these and other items.

Emerson has done much toward identifying the characteristics of objects that make them valuable in exchanges. Need, uncertainty, and reinforcement capacity clearly influence the value of objects in exchanges. Unfortunately, need and uncertainty are not as objective nor concrete as Emerson suggests. Cultures may transmit general evaluations of the need and uncertainty surrounding various objects, but individuals internalize these collective evaluations to different degrees (Mobley et al, 1982; Hegtvedt, 1988). The type of exchange relationship, and employees' perceptions and evaluations of resources received in these exchange relationships also affect their value. The need attached to an input may appear objective to scientific investigators, but there is no guarantee that individuals are equally aware of the objective value attached to various resources.

Assessing the biological (or psychological) need for given resources requires that individuals make subjective evaluations about their immediate and long-term desires (Cook, 1975), and this may influence which resources have value in exchange relationships (cf. Thibaut and Kelley, 1959). Finally, understanding the value of resources transferred through transactions is not possible without knowledge of which resources are conditioned or generalized reinforcements for employees. This determination is more straightforward for some resources than it is for others. Under normal circumstances, money is a generalized reinforcement because it can be converted into a great variety of resources. The reinforcement qualities of more abstract objects such as the amount of autonomy an employee has or the level and quality of interaction they share with superiors are far less clear. Currently, research assumes that employees perceive these job characteristics uniformly (Price, 1977; Mobley et al., 1979).

In short, value is a social *and* an individual abstraction. Therefore, research that assesses the value of resources against objective benchmarks is, at best, ambiguous. The same should apply to assessments of job characteristics used to evaluate employee satisfaction and commitment (Mobley, 1982), organizational constraints (Price, 1977), and investments (Farrell and Rusbult, 1981; Rusbult and Farrell, 1983). Since individuals also place value on exchange resources completely beyond the range of normative prescripts, value must be partly subjective. Previous research does not properly identify which job and organizational characteristics employees evaluate as costs and rewards, nor how much value employees attribute to these resources.

Herzberg's (1974) influential work that distinguishes between work conditions that cause dissatisfaction and satisfaction contributes much toward defining the relationship between job characteristics and job attitudes. He argues that work conditions that relate to how people are treated, the job context, are sources of dissatisfaction (e.g., supervision by others, company policy and administrative practices, interpersonal relationships, and salary). Work conditions that relate to the content of jobs produce satisfaction (e.g., achievement, recognition for achievement, and the work itself). It is common to see these "job events" characterized as determinants of job satisfaction in turnover models (Price, 1977). Herzberg's treatment of job characteristics represents a fundamental advancement in identifying the determinants of workplace behavior. However, he too holds true to the basic tenet of research on job characteristics, and assumes that job characteristics have a universal effect on all employees. I argue that the value contained in exchange resources cannot be ascertained without knowledge of the subjective interpretations and evaluations that workers place on these resources.

Social exchange theory should realize that reinforcements do not derive solely from normative prescripts (e.g., income, social approval). Personality traits filter perceptions of reinforcements in different situations (Endler and Magnusson, 1976). Psychological needs and dispositions also affect individual evaluations of rewards and costs (Blau, 1964:20). A model of quitting behavior that follows from social exchange theory could incorporate all of these ideas. Such a model would argue that individuals are engaged in exchange relations with organizational actors that provide reinforcement for work related behaviors. Social exchange theory could then provide a better explanation of behavior by considering the context where they occur *and* the contextual factors that are salient to individuals (Blau, 1964). Work occurs within organizations that vary extensively, and jobs encompass prestigious, socially inconsequential, arduous, routine, and exciting activities. How individuals interpret and evaluate these varied characteristics of work is an empirical question.

When applied to quitting behavior, exchange theory avoids the workplace and marketplace determinism in traditional economic and sociological theory on quitting behavior by specifying a broader range of exchange resources than have been identified in previous models. Moreover, social exchange theory is flexible enough to incorporate personality effects. With these advantages, and a more inclusive definition of turnover, research can begin to uncover subtle nuances in the person × work-domain interaction that determine quitting behavior. Turnover and quitting behavior are used interchangeably in the remainder of this paper to refer to voluntary transfers and quits.

The present research contributes to work on employee turnover by examining the person × work-domain interaction. It also extends previous work on exchanges by showing that individuals organize work conditions in their environment into categories of costs and rewards, and make decisions about their actions based on personality characteristics. Explaining behavior in organizations involves understanding how behaviors and reinforcements are integrated into a framework that meets the needs and wishes of employees and employers. Employees whose work environments do not meet their material and psychological needs tend to leave, if alternatives are available (Emerson, 1972). Moreover, jobs that offer few benefits but contain many costs may be abandoned despite perceived opportunity, if the job is not crucial to maintaining individual or family lifestyles.

Emerson (1972) argues that organizations are actors in exchange relations. Employees also maintain exchange relations with supervisors, coworkers, and clients. Examining these relationships will test for the person × work-domain interaction, and determine its impact on quitting behavior. According to the social exchange approach outlined above, quitting behavior occurs if employees perceive that staying with their current employment relationship (i.e., work conditions) costs more than switching to another employment relationship. The distinguishing feature of this analysis of work conditions and quitting behavior is the use of personality to define the relative cost and reward value of work conditions.

HYPOTHESES

The first step in identifying the significant factors associated with employee quitting decisions is to discover which work conditions are salient to individual employees. Of all the personality constructs used in previous turnover research, LOC is alone in providing a theoretical basis for distinguishing the salience of specific work characteristics among personality types, and determining which drive behavior (Rotter, 1966; Lefcourt, 1982; Staw et al,. 1986). LOC theory asserts that internals perceive more control over their environment, are less likely to experience stress under stressful conditions, manage interpersonal relationships better, and are more goal-directed than externals. Two hypotheses follow from this knowledge. The first derives from understanding which factors are salient among internals and externals, and the second from understanding which factors are likely to be perceived as costs and rewards.

H1:   Internals and externals have different perceptions of the same work conditions. Internals will perceive more job autonomy, intensity of work load, more routine tasks, and positive interpersonal relationships than externals.

H2:   Personality affects the rewards, costs, and profit that employees receive from the work relationship. Job autonomy, communication about job events, interpersonal relationships with coworkers and supervisors will contribute more to job rewards among internals than externals. Routine job tasks, work loads, and low job autonomy will contribute more to job costs among internals than externals.

A significant reinforcement in most employment relationships is compensation. Given that internals are more goal-directed than externals, have a greater tolerance for stress, and perceive more control over their environment (Rotter, 1966; Andrisani and Nestel, 1976; O'Brien, 1984), they will be more likely to feel accountable, in part, for the amount of resources they receive on the job and to increase work output to achieve equity. Externals, however, are less likely to believe that they can affect work outcomes and will be more likely to limit output under similar conditions. Thus, externals are more likely to exhibit behavior that is consistent with an exchange orientation than are internals.

H3:   Externals will have stronger exchange ideologies than internals.

My final two hypotheses derive from exchange theory (Thibaut and Kelly, 1959; Blau, 1964; Rusbult, 1980; Emerson, 1981) and LOC theory, and describe when employees will leave employment relationships and how personalty affects their decision.

H4:   Employees who perceive that the costs associated with their jobs outweigh the rewards they receive are more likely to switch jobs, when they believe that they can obtain more profit from alternative employment relationships. The amount of profit realized in the current employment relationship will have a smaller effect on the odds of quitting among externals.

H5:   Exchange ideology is positively related to quitting when job costs outweigh job rewards, and when employees perceive that alternatives exist.

Previous research does not consider workplace behavior in terms of exchanges between employees, organizations, coworkers, supervisors, and customers. Each of these exchange relationships contain costs and rewards; this situation suggests several new problems for students of workplace behavior. First, does having varying levels of exposure to the resources in each of these relationships affect quitting behavior? Second, do employees have preferences for the types of resources that a particular relationship provides? Third, do costs and rewards associated with the more salient relationships have the largest impact on employee decisions to quit or stay? Finally, does a hierarchy of exchange resources or exchange relationships develop with the stronger resources and relationships supplementing the profit deficiencies in the less important ones? Theory of LOC suggests that internals will place more value on the organizational and supervisory relationships, while externals will place more value on co-worker and client relationships. The answers to these questions are essential to gaining a comprehensive understanding of quitting behavior, and they will necessitate revision and rethinking of existing theories of quitting behavior.

II

Methodology

The data with which to analyze turnover derive from a survey of almost 3000 employees of a state level Human Services Agency (HSA). The data were collected in three phases. First, a survey questionnaire was developed which contained some 200 items on employee attitudes and beliefs about work processes, job characteristics, LOC, exchange ideology, and several other work related concepts defined as important determinants of turnover (Price, 1977; Mobley et. al., 1979; Muchinsky and Tuttle, 1979; Farrell and Rusbult, 1981: Spector and Michaels, 1986). Variables used in this analysis appear in Appendix A. One hundred employees were randomly selected from the target population to participate in a pilot-test of the questionnaire. Results of the pilot study (not shown here) suggested that the questions were clear to the HSA employees; after making minor adjustments the tool was administered to the remaining employees in the target occupations. The study population consisted of the 2846 social counselors, eligibility counselors, disability claims examiners, and vocational rehabilitation counselors employed by HSA in June, 1989.

Second, each employee in the study population received a packet containing a cover letter from the Commissioner of Human Services, a questionnaire, and a pre-addressed and stamped return envelope. The cover letter stated the purpose of the study, described the professional and organizational affiliation of members on the Turnover Study Project Team, notified participants that they could complete the questionnaire during their work shifts, and gave employees assurances of confidentiality. Demographic data from employees' Personnel Department files were merged with the questionnaire data. Third, HSA recorded the first turnover event each employee experienced between June, 1989 and July 1990.

Dependent Variable

Most practitioners of turnover research define turnover as movement across the boundaries of an organization—or quitting (Price, 1977). I define turnover as any voluntary movement out of a job. This includes quits, transfers, and promotions, for two reasons. First, job and work characteristics identified in previous research as determinants of "turnover" also explain variation in transfers (Tudor and Dalton, 1986). Second, defining turnover as movement across organizational boundaries suggests that this behavior is independent of movement occurring within organizational boundaries. These arguments suggest that the findings in previous research may be skewed. They also suggest that variables purported to be determinants of "turnover" in previous research may not affect quitting, as traditionally defined.

Coding the turnover variable according to Price's definition would result in categorizing all employees who left organizational boundaries as quitters and all employees who remained within organizational boundaries, despite their mobility within the firm, as stayers. Under this coding scheme, employees who transfer or receive promotions are classified as stayers. Research comparing job turnover to company turnover suggests that when transfers are grouped with stayers, the question being answered concerns which explanatory variables explain the odds of quitting compared with staying *or* changing jobs within the organization. Obviously, the behaviors being contrasted here involve multiple events—ignoring this distorts reality. Perhaps less obvious is that ignoring this reality may distort the observed effects of explanatory variables on the odds of leaving a job. Therefore, it is important to examine turnover by contrasting homogeneous groups of employees, based on their having experienced similar types of turnover.

If turnover is a process (Greenhalgh, 1980), then research must analyze its causes among discrete events. Employees have a repertoire of turnover options that include transferring, promoting, and quitting that could represent rational decision making and planning toward career goals. Ignoring the turnover process and the possible sequencing of promotions, transfers, and quits could mislead conclusions about the nature of turnover despite the definition used. Therefore, employees who experience transfers or promotions should be analyzed separately from quits.

Independent Variables

Locus of Control theory describes how personality types might perceive work conditions (Rotter, 1966; Lefcourt, 1983), and figures prominently in recent work on employee turnover (Spector, 1982; Spector and Michaels, 1986; Griffeth and Hom, 1988). The validity of the LOC construct has been tested among undifferentiated populations (Mirels, 1970; Lumpkin, 1985; Goodman and Waters, 1987), and across ethnic populations (Garza and Widlak, 1977). Rotter's (1966) measurement of LOC, the standard used in previous research, is used in the present study.

Scores on the LOC scale ranged from zero, if respondents selected the internal option for each of the twenty-three items in the scale, to a score of twenty-three if the external option was selected for each item. Table 1 lists descriptive statistics for LOC and the other independent variables used in this analysis.

The LOC scale has an alpha reliability coefficient of .75, and a mean score of 9.3, showing that the average worker has an internal LOC. The scale has a standard deviation of 3.9. Twelve percent of the study sample scores from 0 to 5, forty-three percent score between 5.1 and 10, thirty-five percent score between 10.1 and 15, nine percent score between 15.1 and 20, and about one percent score between 20.1 and 23. Seventy-two percent of the study sample is mathematically classified as internals (with scores of 11.5 or below).

Exchange Ideology comprises five items measuring the extent to which respondents agree or disagree with exchange principles (these items are from Eisenberger et al. [1986]). Two important reasons exist for analyzing exchange ideology in this study: first, exchange ideology is a direct link between employees' rational evaluations of performance-compensation ratios and turnover decisions; second, exchange ideology is related to LOC—internals have greater expectations that effort will lead to good performance and that good performance will produce rewards (Spector, 1982). Distinguishing the effects of exchange ideology from the more generalized component of personality, LOC, will be important.

Table 1. Means, Standard Deviations, and Reliability Coefficients for Independent Variables.

Variables	Mean	SD	Alpha
Age (in years)	38.4	10.2	—
Tenure (in years)	7.4	6.7	—
LOC	9.3	3.9	.75
Exchange Ideology	1.9	1.4	.64
Manageability of Caseload	3.8	1.8	.76
% of routine tasks	10.5	2.9	.83
Job autonomy	7.3	1.7	.65
Formal communication	12.7	2.9	.81
Supervisor encouragement	21.7	4.0	.87
Supervisor age-, sex-, race-bias	3.8	1.8	.78
Coworkers encouragement	21.1	3.9	.83
Coworker age-, sex-, race-bias	3.8	1.9	.81
Client deservedness[a]	−.01	2.9	.77
Job costs	4.5	1.8	—
Job rewards	5.3	1.7	—
Profit	1.0	2.8	—
Comparison level	1.5	.6	—
Ease of finding another job	3.3	1.1	—
Job satisfaction	9.1	2.2	.87
Job commitment	2.1	.9	—

a. The items used to construct this scale have been standardized to have a mean of 0 and a standard deviation of 1.

Scores on the exchange ideology scale range from a high of 5, meaning that the respondent chose the exchange oriented response for each of the five items, to 0, if the exchange oriented response was never selected. The scale mean, standard deviation, and alpha reliability coefficient are 1.94, 1.44, and .64, respectively. Eighty-three percent of the respondents score between 0 and 3; each one point increment in the exchange ideology score encompasses approximately 20% of the distribution. The mean score on this scale suggests that the average employee has a low exchange orientation.

Theory that explains how LOC and exchange ideology affect work conditions and job attitudes suggests that employees view work conditions as exchange resources and that job satisfaction, rewards, and costs reflect their evaluation of these resources (Price, 1977; Rusbult and Farrell, 1983). That is, personality affects how employees perceive and evaluate centralization, case load size, routine tasks, formal communication, interpersonal relationships, job rewards and job costs, job satisfaction, job commitment, and job profit. Conceptualization and measurement of the resources exchanged in the work relationships and job attitudes are described next.

Several influential writers use the exchange resources and job attitudes described above to model employee turnover (for review articles see March and Simon, 1957; Price, 1977; Bluedorn, 1982; Mobley et al., 1982). These variables are used in the present study to permit comparison of competing models, or important segments of these competing models. I now describe how resources, values, and job attitudes are measured in previous research and in the present study.

Price (1977) argues that pay, integration, instrumental communication, and formal communication are positively correlated with job satisfaction, and that centralization of power within firms and job satisfaction are negatively associated. Moreover, job satisfaction and alternative employment options affect employee turnover decisions. According to Price and Mueller (1986), integration is the extent of participation in primary relationships; instrumental communication is information that relates to role performance; formal communication refers to officially transmitted information; and centralization is the degree that power is centralized within organizations.

Integration. I use Price and Mueller's definition for this resource; here, however, it is operationalized to obtain a more comprehensive measurement of the concept. Integration is measured with four scales: two measure the extent to which primary relationships between employees and supervisors, and between employees and non-supervisory coworkers, are encouraging and respectful (hereafter called supervisor encouragement and coworker encouragement, respectively); two other scales measure the extent of supervisor and non-supervisory coworker age-, race-, and sex-bias present in primary relationships (hereafter called supervisor and coworker bias,).

Generally, employees report uniformly high levels of supervisor and coworker encouragement. Both scales range from 5 to 24, with higher scores reflecting greater encouragement. The supervisor and coworker encouragement scales have means of 21.71 and 21.12, standard deviations of 4.0 and 3.87, and alpha reliability coefficients of .87 and .83, respectively. Employees also report uniformly low levels of supervisor and coworker bias.

Client Deservedness. Satisfaction in knowing that one's efforts achieve their desired goals is an important reinforcement. HSA's goals include matching clients to services, and to helping clients achieve economic, physical, and psychological independence. Obviously, client performance is critical to this goal. Should clients achieve only modest progress toward economic and social independence rather than total independence, human service workers will likely perceive their involvement as rewarding. If, on the other hand, clients do not progress for reasons perceived by human service workers as a lack of effort, human service workers will tend to perceive their involvement with clients as costly. This idea is captured in human service workers' assessments of how deserving their clients are of HSA services. The concept is measured by asking HSA employees to comment on several behavioral and attitudinal characteristics of their clients. Since the items measuring client deservedness have different response ranges, each was first standardized to have a mean of 0 and a standard deviation of 1 before they were combined to create the client deservedness scale. Consequently, the scale also has a mean of 0 and a standard deviation of 1.

Formal Communication. Communication is also measured to maximize the richness of Price and Mueller's definition of the concept. This is accomplished by creating a scale composed of 5 items reflecting the extent of officially transmitted information about procedures related to role performance, job benefits, and social activities—thus more than meeting the criteria these authors use to define instrumental *and* formal communication. I call this variable formal communication because the information is transmitted through official channels. The formal communication scale ranges from 4 to 16, with higher scores reflecting lower levels of perceived formal communication. The scale mean is 12.68; the standard deviation is 2.88; the alpha reliability coefficient is .81.

Job Autonomy. Price and Mueller define centralization as the level of power stratification within organizations; they measure the concept as the number of workers at different organizational levels who participate in making organizational decisions. Others define centralization as the extent of say that workers have over aspects of work (Thompson and Terpening, 1983). The two definitions are substantively equivalent—the first pertaining to macro level phenomena while the latter refers to micro level phenomena. Since individuals' perceptions are central to this research, I call this concept job autonomy. The job autonomy scale is measured with two items and ranges from 2 to 10, with higher scores reflecting high job autonomy. The scale has a mean of 7.28, a standard deviation of 1.73, and an alpha reliability coefficient of .65.

Routinization. Task routinization is not used in Price's model of turnover, although some researchers consider the concept an important determinant of dissatisfaction (Thompson and Terpening, 1983). Perceptions of routinization are hypothesized to interact with personality and affect evaluations of job costs and job rewards (Rotter, 1966). The routinization scale is measured with 2 items and ranges from 2 to 14, with higher scores reflecting high task routinization. The scale has a mean of 10.48, a standard deviation of 2.89, and an alpha reliability coefficient of .83.

Job Satisfaction. Job satisfaction is a determinant of turnover common to Price (1977) and Mobley (1982). Price (1977:79) views job satisfaction as the degree to which employees have a positive attitudinal orientation toward employment in their organizations. Mobley (1982:125), having a broader view, argues that satisfaction is a present-oriented evaluation of employees' values and the benefits they perceive the organization offers. According to Price and Mobley, then, satisfaction is a global measure of employees' positive affect toward the job and organization.

Job satisfaction was measured using 4 items with Likert response formats that were combined into a summated rating scale (Rusbult and Farrell, 1983; Price and Mueller, 1986). The job satisfaction scale ranges from a low of 4 to a high of 16; and, has a mean of 9.1, a standard deviation of 2.5, and an alpha reliability coefficient of .87.

Job Commitment. Job commitment refers to a desire to remain an employee of the organization (Mowday et al., 1982), or a psychological attachment to one's job (Rusbult and Farrell, 1983). These definitions represent attitudinal and behavioral dimensions of commitment (O'Reilly and Caldwell, 1981). Price and Mueller (1986) suggest that both dimensions refer to organizational loyalty. I use the behavioral oriented measure of commitment that reflects employee behavioral intentions. The item asks: "How committed are you to staying with your job?", and ranges from 1 "very committed" to 4 "not at all committed": The mean job commitment score for the study sample is 2.1 and the standard deviation is .89.

Rewards, Costs and Profit. Rewards and costs represent the reinforcement characteristics of employees' work experiences. According to exchange theory, employees who receive positive reinforcement from work experiences tend to maintain the behavior that generated those rewards. Employees who receive negative reinforcement from work experiences tend to extinguish the behavior that generated those costs. Rewards and costs were measured as the extent to which jobs involve positive and negative experiences (Thompson and Terpening, 1983). Profit is equal to rewards minus costs and represents the net value employees derive from their jobs. According to exchange theory, work experiences that provide more negative reinforcement than positive reinforcement yield no profit and are at risk of termination.

Job reward and job cost scores range from 1 to 9—high scores means high rewards and costs. The mean reward score for the study sample is 5.3 and the standard deviation is 1.7. The corresponding mean cost score is 4.5 and the standard deviation is 1.8. The mean profit (rewards minus costs) score is .97, and the standard deviation of 2.8.

Comparison Level. Comparison Level (CL) refers to the standard against which employees compare rewards and costs that derive from their work experience (Thibaut and Kelly, 1959). Therefore, it represents the average value of outcomes that employees have come to expect from their employment relationship. Employees who believe they can derive more value from a different employment relationship are at risk of terminating their current employment relationship for a better alternative. Comparison level was measured in terms of employees perceiving more or fewer negative features than most people have in their employment relationships. The mean CL score is 2.6 (the range is between 1 and 3); the standard deviation is 2.5. The average employee believes that their job has fewer negative features than most people have at their places of employment.

Opportunity. Sociological, psychological, and exchange theories use alternative job opportunity to model turnover (March and Simons, 1958; Price, 1977; Bluedorn,1982; Mobley, 1982; Rusbult and Farrell, 1983). Opportunity is defined as an employee's perception of the ease of movement from his or her current job to an alternative job (March and Simons, 1958; Mobley, 1982) or the availability of alternative jobs (Price, 1977; Bluedorn, 1982; Rusbult and Farrell, 1983). I measure employees' perceptions of the ease of finding alternative work (Thompson and Terpening). On average, employees say that finding a job with another employer would be "somewhat difficult" to "very difficult." The mean score is 3.3 on a scale that ranges from 1 to 4—higher scores reflect less opportunity; the standard deviation is 1.1.

Analysis of Non-Response

Eighteen hundred and seventeen employees, 64 percent, of the 2846 workers in the study population returned a completed questionnaire. Table 2 lists the distributions on demographic variables for respondents and non-respondents. Fifty-four percent (984) of respondents are eligibility counselors, 35 percent (637) are social counselors, 7 percent (127) are vocational rehabilitation specialists, and 4 percent (70) are disability claims examiners. The proportion of employees occupying these positions in HSA is 57 percent, 33 percent, 6 percent, and 4 percent, respectively.

Eighty percent of all respondents are female and 81 percent are white, while 80 percent of the study population is female and 74 percent are white. The average age of respondents and employees in the study population is 38 years. The average length of service for respondents and members of the study population is 7.1 and 7.4 years, respectively. The analysis of demographic attributes of respondents and non-respondents reveals that non-whites, social counselors, and eligibility counselors are under-represented in the study sample; this group also has less tenure on average. The small size of these discrepancies would not appear to constitute a significant response bias.

Table 3 shows frequency distributions on turnover for respondents and non-respondents. Respondents accounted for three hundred and eighty-nine transfers, promotions, and resignations between June, 1989 and July, 1990. These numbers reflect twenty-one percent turnover among respondents. The study population is also experienced twenty-one percent turnover. Quitting is the most common turnover event for respondents and employees in the study population, accounting for fifty-five percent of the turnover in both groups. Transfers accounted for thirty-seven percent of the turnover among respondents and thirty-eight percent overall. Eight percent of the turnover among respondents and the population occurred through promotion. The distribution of quits, transfers, and promotions among respondents and the study population suggests that turnover among respondents is representative of turnover in the study population.

To further test for response bias on the dependent variable, I conducted a logistic regression of response status (ie., respondents and non-respondents) on type of turnover, race, sex, region, marital status, and job title (see Table 4). The results show that, when other variables in the equation are held constant, the type of turnover event does not affect the odds of returning a questionnaire enough to reject the null hypothesis of independence at the .05 level. These multivariate results are even stronger

Table 2. Distribution of Region, Marital Status, Sex, Race, and Job Title for Respondents and Non-respondents

Variable	Respondents n (%)	Non-respondents n (%)
Region		
0	92 (05)	55 (05)
1	164 (09)	61 (06)
2	209 (12)	121 (12)
3	97 (05)	24 (02)
4	104 (06)	29 (03)
5	150 (08)	78 (08)
6	119 (07)	34 (03)
7	111 (06)	25 (02)
8	131 (07)	56 (06)
19	174 (10)	99 (10)
33	91 (05)	82 (08)
47	79 (04)	107 (10)
79	296 (16)	258 (25)
Marital status		
Divorced	119 (07)	58 (05)
Married	1170 (64)	637 (62)
Separated	16 (01)	20 (02)
Single	495 (27)	308 (30)
Widowed	17 (01)	6 (01)
Sex		
Female	1448 (80)	831 (81)
Male	369 (20)	198 (19)
Race		
Non-white	355 (20)	380 (37)
White	1462 (80)	649 (63)
Occupation		
Disability claims examiner	70 (04)	49 (05)
Eligibility counselor	983 (54)	629 (61)
Social counselor	637 (35)	315 (31)
Vocational Rehabilitation counselor	127 (07)	36 (03)

support that turnover among respondents is representative of turnover among employees in the study population.

Gender, job tenure, age, salary, and marital status do not affect the odds of returning a questionnaire. However, non-whites and employees in region 2, 33, and 47 are under-represented; while social counselors and vocational rehabilitation counselors, and region 7 are over-represented in the study sample.

The analysis of response bias shows that the study sample is not representative of the population with respect to race, region, and occupation. Previous work does not explore the effects of race on turnover. Of the three studies I reviewed that considered urban-rural effects, one found less turnover in rural areas. These findings suggest that caution should be taken in interpreting the results of race and region effects. Previous research has not examined the effect of different occupations on turnover rates. Finally, no empirical evidence exists to show that race and geographic region have a significant effect on perceptions of work conditions or personality. The next section examines the data for potential problems that might result from using highly correlated independent variables.

Table 3. Distributions on Type of Turnover by Respondents and Non-respondents

Dependent variables	Respondents N (%)	Non-respondents N (%)
Type of turnover		
No turnover	1429 (78)	814 (79)
Promotion	30 (02)	15 (02)
Transfer	145 (08)	82 (08)
Resignation	214 (12)	116 (11)
Total	1817 (64)	1029 (36)

Table 4. Logistic Regression of the Odds of Returning a Questionnaire[a]

Independent variables	Metric regression coefficients
Turnover status[b]	
Promotion	−.069
Demotion	.348
Transfer	.236
Quit	−.189
Tenure in current job (in years)	.001
Job[b]	
Disability claims examiner	−.321
Social counselor	.267*
Vocational rehabilitation counselor	.787*
Region[b]	
0	.034
1	.074
2	−.390*
3	.510
4	.329
5	−.299
6	.368
7	.614*
8	.082
33	−.581*
47	1.242*
79	−.166
Race (White=1)	−.817*
Sex (Female=1)	−.040
Age (in years)	.001
Salary, annual ($)	.000
Constant	1.159
Improvement in chi-square	236.7*
Percentage of cases correctly predicted=	66.8

a. Coefficients for marital status did not obtain statistical significance and are not shown here.

b. The benchmark categories are: turnover status, remained in same job; job, eligibility counselor; region, region 19.

* $p \leq .05$

Analysis of Multicollinearity

This study examines the effect of 18 exchange resources, job attitudes, and personality variables, each contextually linked to the workplace, on turnover. Logistic regression results may be distorted if highly correlated independent variables appear in the same regression equation. This condition, called multicollinearity, is problematic because highly correlated independent variables contribute competing or overlapping effects to the dependent variable. Haydak (1987:176) argues that the magnitude of the correlation between variables that is problematic depends on the research; generally, however, variables whose zero-order correlations exceed .8 exhibit multicollinearity.

The work experience of social, eligibility, and vocational rehabilitation counselors and disability claims examiners involve daily transactions between co-workers, supervisors, and the actor-organization. Table 5 shows zero-order correlations for all independent variables used in this analysis of turnover. Most zero-order correlations between demographic characteristics, exchange partnerships, and job attitudes are statistically significant. However, none of these correlations exceed .8 (the strongest correlation is .58).

Summary

This chapter describes the study population, respondents, and the variables to be used in the following chapters to examine quitting behavior. The study population consists of almost 3000 disability claims examiners and social, eligibility, and vocational rehabilitation counselors employed by HSA. Sixty-four percent of these employees completed a questionnaire that measured more than 200 job-related, personality and attitudinal variables. Demographic information was obtained from Personnel Department records, and employees' turnover status was collected over one year. These data were then merged into the study data file.

Analyses of response bias and multicollinearity attest to the good quality of the study data. The data does contain minor response bias with respect to race, region, and occupation, suggesting that caution should be exercised when using these variables to model turnover. That is, there is little consensus or precedent for understanding how these variables affect turnover decisions. Eighteen job-related, personality, attitudinal and demographic variables that constitute several important models of turnover are examined in this analysis of turnover. These variables were measured using items employed in previous turnover studies to facilitate testing between turnover models. Results of means tests and regression analysis show that the inter-item correlations between the independent variables used in this study are not problematic.

Table 5. Zero-order Correlations Among Independent Variables

	1	2	3	4	5	6	7	8	9	10
1. Locus of control	1.000									
2. Exchange ideology	.138*	1.000								
3. Age (in years)	-.117*	-.062*	1.000							
4. Tenure (in years)	-.069*	.012	.576*	1.000						
5. Manageability of case load	-.074*	-.057*	-.013	-.020	1.000					
6. % routine tasks	.081*	.067*	.050*	.123*	.006	1.000				
7. Job autonomy	-.007	-.110*	-.012	.005	-.161*	-.108*	1.000			
8. Supervisor support	-.100*	-.028	-.045*	-.032	.085*	-.013	.187*	1.000		
9. Supervisor age, sex, race-bias	.060*	.051*	.018	-.020	-.022	.009	-.148*	-.418*	1.000	
10. Coworker support	-.150*	-.013	-.035	-.054*	-.040	-.052*	.092*	.237*	-.154*	1.000
11. Coworker age, sex, race-bias	.054*	.035	.008	-.045*	.044	.026	-.079*	-.135*	.522*	-.226*
12. Client deservedness	-.162*	-.118*	.079*	.065*	.188*	-.127*	.128*	.067*	-.006	.066*
13. Comparison level	-.114*	-.038*	.125*	.125*	.278*	.059*	.172*	.171*	-.061*	.096
14. % pleasant experiences	-.163*	-.092*	.194*	.173*	.245*	-.084*	.265*	.152*	-.041	.100*
15. % unpleasant experiences	.143*	.100*	-.214*	-.182*	-.294*	-.086*	-.190*	-.138*	.106*	-.069*
16. Formal communication	.104*	.020	-.071*	-.113	-.097*	.044*	-.164*	-.254*	.123*	-.183*

Table 5. Zero-order Correlations Among Independent Variables

	11	12	13	14	15	16
11. Coworker age, sex, race-bias	1.000					
12. Client deservedness	-.024	1.000				
13. Comparison level	-.031*	.202*	1.000			
14. Job rewards	-.018	.336*	-.169*	1.000		
15. Job costs	.084*	-.452*	.138*	-.411*	1.000	
16. Formal communication	.098*	-.064	-.201*	-.229*	.182*	1.000

* p <= .05.

III

Personality, Exchange Resources and Quitting

The relationship between personality, work conditions, and turnover will be examined in the context of workplace exchange relationships. These relationships exist between employees and four organizational actors: supervisors, coworkers, the organization, and clients. Employees exchange their labor, skills, and talents for the salary, benefits, job responsibilities, encouragement, and professional respect that supervisors and the organization provide. They also exchange encouragement and professional respect with coworkers. And they exchange their efforts, pride in moral and professional achievement for the self-helping behaviors that clients bring to the relationship. Personality affects employees' perceptions of these resources, their evaluations of the reinforcement value of these exchange resources, and quitting behavior.

T-tests, zero-order correlation, ordinary least squares regression, and logistic regression analyses are used to examine personality effects on perceptions of resources, the reinforcement value of these resources, and the reinforcement value × personality interaction effect on quitting. The remainder of this chapter is organized as follows. First, I use the t-test and ordinary least squares (OLS) regression to examine how internals and externals perceive exchange resources. Second, I use correlation analysis to examine the statistical association between exchange ideology and exchange resources, and between exchange ideology and LOC. Third, I regress job costs, rewards, and profit on exchange resources within four LOC groups to determine the reinforcement qualities of exchange resources. Finally, I use logistic regression to model the effects of job profit, comparison level, alternative opportunity, LOC, and exchange ideology on the odds of quitting.

Personality and Exchange Resources

My first hypothesis states that LOC significantly influences employees' perceptions of exchange resources. LOC theory posits that internals will perceive more autonomy in the workplace, will value flexibility in job tasks, and by virtue of interpersonal skills will form more constructive social relations than externals (Rotter, 1966). Internals will also tend to receive more reinforcement from these exchange resources. The effect of LOC on employees' attitudes toward their clients has not been examined, but internals, who tend to be goal-directed and believe in personal agency, may judge recipients of social services more harshly than externals. The variation in externals' and internals' perceptions of exchange resources is examined by comparing mean scores on exchange resources.

Table 6 shows mean scores on exchange resources for the sample, internals, and externals, and the results of a t-test of the difference between the means for internals and externals. The mean scores on each resource traded in supervisor, coworker, client, and organizational exchange relationships differ significantly for internals and externals (at $p<.05$). Internals describe their case loads as more manageable than externals, and they perceive more job autonomy and formal communication than externals. The perception that clients deserve the services they receive, and that supervisors and coworkers are encouraging is stronger among internals. Internals perceive more instrumental exchange resources than externals. These resources tend to have a direct impact on job performance. Externals score higher than internals on qualitative (or intrinsic) job characteristics; they perceive more routine in their work, and report that supervisors and coworkers hold more age-, race-, or sex-biases against them than internals. The differences observed in the means of exchange resources support my first hypothesis. Externals perceive less autonomy in the workplace and exhibit less instrumental behavior than internals; they perceive more qualitative job characteristics such as variation in job tasks and respectful interpersonal relations. Internals tend to perceive more control over their work environment than externals; they also exhibit more instrumental behavior than externals. Since the structural position that supervisors hold within the organization provides supervisors with some influence over how successfully subordinates can perform their jobs, it follows that internals would develop supportive relationships with supervisors. Internals also perceive more positive interpersonal exchanges with coworkers than externals. This probably reflects the advantage that internals enjoy over externals in controlling social relationships (Rotter, 1966).

Table 6. Means on Exchange Resources and Job Attitudes by LOC

Variables	Means*		
	Total sample	Internals	Externals
Resources:			
Manageability of caseload	3.8	3.9	3.6
Formal communication	12.7	12.5	13.1
% of routine tasks	10.5	10.4	10.7
Job autonomy	7.2	7.3	7.0
Supervisor encouragement	21.7	21.9	21.2
Supervisor age-, sex-, race-bias	3.8	3.8	4.0
Coworker encouragement	21.1	21.3	20.5
Coworker age-, sex-, race-bias	3.8	3.8	4.0
Client deservedness[a]	−.0	.2	−.5
Job attitudes:			
Job costs	4.5	4.4	4.8
Job rewards	5.3	5.4	5.0
Profit (difference of positive and negative job experiences)	.8	1.0	.2
Comparison level	1.5	1.5	1.5
Ease of finding another job	3.3	3.3	3.1
Job satisfaction	9.1	9.0	9.5
Job commitment	2.1	2.0	2.2

a. The items used to construct scale were standardized to have a mean of 0 and a standard deviation of 1.
* All internal-external differences in means are significant at $p \leq .05$.

My second hypothesis states that internals perceive more positive interpersonal relations with supervisors than with coworkers who are in structurally equivalent positions because the worker-supervisor relationship offers greater profit making potential. However, the difference in the mean scores on supervisor encouragement *and* coworker encouragement for internals and externals are equally significant—internals score about .8 higher than externals on both resources.

The evidence shows that internals do promote supportive relationships with supervisors. However, it appears that the emphasis is on nurturing exchange relationships in general and not solely with exchange partners who are in superior positions—this propensity extends to non-supervisory coworkers. Internals' perceptions of more constructive exchange relationships with coworkers and supervisors may reflect greater confidence in their ability to influence situations, and a greater capacity to exert control over the work process through exchange relationships. Overall, the evidence from comparing mean scores on exchange resources for internals and externals supports my second hypothesis.

My third hypothesis addresses the relationship between exchange ideology, LOC, and exchange resources. The results of the correlation analysis of personality and exchange resources appear in Table 5. The correlation coefficient for LOC and exchange ideology is a modest but statistically significant .14. Externals have a greater exchange ideology score than internals. In fact, internals have a mean of 1.8 on the exchange ideology scale compared to externals' 2.3, and this difference is significant at P<= .001. This finding supports my third hypothesis. The results in Table 5 reveal that stronger associations exist between exchange resources and LOC than between exchange ideology and exchange resources. Each resource exchanged in person-supervisor and person-coworker exchanges has a strong statistically significant correlation with LOC; only one resource is significantly associated with exchange ideology. There is a small positive association between exchange ideology and perceptions that supervisors have age-, race-, and sex-biases.

Externals and high exchange oriented individuals are more likely than their counterparts to say that their case loads are beyond their ability to manage effectively, that they have little autonomy over their jobs, and that their job tasks are routine. Compared to internals and low exchange oriented individuals, externals and high exchange oriented individuals also tend to say that their clients do not deserve the services they receive from HSA.

These results suggest that LOC affects a broader range of exchange resources than does exchange ideology. Exchange ideology primarily affects perceptions of resources in person-organization exchanges (e.g., job tasks) rather than resources exchanged between supervisors, coworkers, or clients. Clearly, LOC and exchange ideology affect perceptions of work conditions and, thus, should be useful in predicting workplace behavior. However, the two concepts are not equally useful. Since LOC is associated with more exchange resources than exchange ideology, it should be a better predictor of turnover than exchange ideology. LOC appears to affect exchange resources in general while exchange ideology primarily affects perceptions of instrumental exchange resources.

Analysis of means and zero-order correlations provide compelling evidence that internals, externals, and high and low exchange oriented employees perceive work conditions differently. However, the mean comparisons do not rule out the possibility that these observed relationships are spurious. To test for spuriousness, each exchange resource is next regressed on personality variables and demographic characteristics.

Regression of Exchange Resources on Personality

To determine if the personality x work-domain interaction affects quitting decisions, I first regress exchange resources on LOC, exchange ideology, and several relevant demographic control variables (Price, 1977). LOC is coded as a dummy variable so that internals can be compared to externals—internals are the omitted category in the regressions. Failure of LOC and exchange ideology effects to reach statistical significance, when occupation, job tenure, salary, age, sex, race, marital status and education are controlled, would show that the significant coefficients derived from correlation analysis are, in fact, spurious. On the other hand, significant regression coefficients for LOC and exchange ideology effects will be taken as further support for my first hypothesis, that personality affects perceptions of work conditions.

Organizational Exchange Resources

In the language of a social exchange theory of turnover, case load size, job tasks, job autonomy, and formal communication are resources exchanged in the person-organization relationship. Table 7 displays standardized regression coefficients from the OLS multiple regression models that test if the relationships between exchange resources, LOC, and exchange ideology are spurious by controlling for other effects that might influence perceptions of exchange resources. The regression results show that externals are more likely than internals to say that their case loads are too heavy for them to manage effectively (.250). Externals also say they receive more routine tasks (.282) than internals. Internals say they receive more job autonomy (–.215), and formal communication (–.839) than externals.

Table 7. OLS Regression of Resources on Locus of Control, Exchange Ideology, and Occupation[a]

Independent variables	Size of case load[b]	Job autonomy	Task routinization	Formal communication[b]	Supervisor support	Supervisor bias	Coworker support	Coworker bias	Client deservedness
LOC (external=1)[c]	.250*	−.215*	.282*	−.839*	−.764*	.247*	−.817*	.217*	−.606*
Exchange ideology	.063*	−.123*	.085*	−.036	−.033	.057	.001[d]	.039	−.204*
Occupation[e]									
Eligibility	.001	−.745*	2.796*	−.158	.337	.032	.014	−.015	−.843*
Vocational	−1.098*	.157	.051	.722	.802*	.024	.642	−.304	1.489*
Disability	−.578*	−.921	1.904*	−1.359*	1.307*	.079	.411	.020	.012
R²	.051*	.066*	.232*	.037*	.028*	.040*	.023*	.062*	.125*

a. Each equation includes 10 control variables whose coefficients are not reported here but are available from the author. These control variables are: job tenure, salary, age, sex, race, marital status (4 dummy variables), and education.

b. Scale reverse coded for consistency—a high score reflects more of the concept measured.

c. In analysis not reported here, 4 dummy variables were created from locus of control score and run in the above equation—the omitted category was high internal. The results showed that locus of control had a linear effect on resources—the dichotomous coding of locus of control is reported for concision.

d. Coefficient multiplied by 1000

e. The omitted benchmark category is social counselor.

* p <= .05

These coefficients show that LOC has a significant effect on perceptions of resources exchanged in the person-organization exchange relationship.

The data also shows statistically significant exchange ideology effects on perceptions of person-organization exchange resources. Employees who have a higher exchange ideology are more likely than employees with lower exchange ideology scores to report that their case load is unmanageable (.063). Employee perceptions of task routinization (.085), and job autonomy (.123) also increase with higher exchange ideology scores. The exchange ideology effect on formal communication is not significant.

The LOC and exchange ideology effects on person-organization exchange resources are significant even when controlling for occupation, job tenure, salary, age, sex, race, marital status, and education.

Supervisor and Coworker Exchange Resources

Resources that employees receive in exchanges with supervisors and non-supervisory coworkers include encouragement, and age-, race-, and sex-bias. Internals say they receive more supervisor encouragement (−.764) and coworker encouragement (−.817) than externals. Externals report receiving more bias than internals from supervisors (.247) and coworkers (.217). In each case, the LOC effect is significant when demographic variables are held constant.

Unlike the coefficients for exchange ideology in the person-organization relationship, the effect of exchange ideology on resources exchanged in the person-supervisor and person-coworker relationships is not significant. The regression results show that the observed zero-order associations between exchange ideology and supervisor and coworker encouragement and bias are spurious. These zero-order associations are explained by LOC and demographic variables.

Client Exchange Resources

Client behaviors that are consistent with the organization's (and employees') goals are resources that clients exchange for the effort that HSA employees expend on their cases—this resource is measured in the client deservedness scale. Internals view their clients as more deserving of HSA services than externals (−.606). Externals tend to believe that their clients could do more to improve their condition if they applied themselves.

Scores on the client deservedness scale also increase as exchange ideology scores decrease (–.204), indicating that high exchange oriented employees tend to hold a more negative view of clients. Employees with a high exchange ideology feel strongly that the benefits one receives should be determined by the effort one expends. These employees may resent clients who they feel are expending too little effort to provide for themselves the services that HSA administers. In this case, these employees are more likely to perceive working with clients as a liability (i.e., cost).

The data show that internals and externals have different perceptions of resources exchanged in each workplace relationship considered above. With regard to the person-organization relationship, externals say that the organization offers more routine job tasks and manageable case loads than internals. Internals report receiving more job autonomy than externals. Internals also receive more encouragement and less bias from supervisors and coworkers than externals. Finally, internals are more likely than externals to characterize their clients as deserving recipients of HSA services.

The results of mean comparisons, zero-order correlation analysis, and OLS regression examined in the preceding section provide strong support for my first and third hypotheses. First, internals and externals perceive workplace exchange resources differently, and they do so as predicted. Second, exchange ideology effects on exchange resources are not significant—suggesting that the observed zero-order correlations are spurious. Third, exchange ideology is related to LOC in the hypothesized direction. Externals have greater exchange ideologies than internals. This is evident from correlation analysis and the similarity in perceptions of exchange resources for externals and employees with high exchange ideology scores.

The evidence showing statistically significant relationships between personality and work conditions presented in this section supports the utility of the LOC construct in distinguishing the positive and negative reinforcement characteristics of resources traded in workplace exchanges. I now examine how employees evaluate workplace exchange resources in terms of job costs, job rewards, and overall job profit.

Exchange Resource Effects on Rewards, Costs and Profit

Examining the reinforcement qualities of exchange resources is best achieved with data that measure employee perceptions of the costs and rewards directly associated with each exchange resource. Absent these observations, the positive and negative reinforcement characteristics (i.e., rewards and costs, respectively) associated with exchange resources can be ascertained empirically. Two global job attitude measures: 1) the level of positive experiences employees have with their jobs (REWARDS); and 2) the proportion of time the job involves unpleasant experiences (COSTS) are examined. Both items are measured on a scale that ranges from 1 (none) to 9 (all). I am assuming that positive experiences are rewarding and negative experiences are costly, and that the two measures reflect employees' assessments of the overall rewards and costs that they derive from their employment relationship. Reinforcement theory suggests that these global evaluations are based on experiences employees have accumulated throughout their tenure at HSA (Fishbein, 1967).

To examine the relationship between LOC, exchange resources, and job costs and job rewards, employees are first mathematically grouped into four personality groups determined by mean and standard deviation scores on the LOC scale. Employees who score more than one standard deviation below the mean are high internals, low internals fall between the mean and one standard deviation below the mean, low externals score between the mean and the mean plus one standard deviation, and high externals fall more than one standard deviation above the mean.

Next, job rewards, job costs and profit are regressed on exchange resources for each LOC sub-group. Significant resource effects on these rewards and costs indicate the positive and negative reinforcement characteristics of resources, while significant resource effects on profit indicate the net reinforcement effect (i.e., value) employees place on exchange resources. Significant differences in these resource effects on reinforcement across personality groups would be evidence of interaction between LOC and exchange resources. That is, internals and externals value different exchange resources *and* place different value on the same exchange resources.

Job Rewards

Table 8 shows the standardized regression coefficients for the regression of rewards, costs, and profit on exchange resources and demographic control variables by personality group. These results show that resources exchanged in the person-organization and person-client relationships have more consistent effects on positive reinforcement than resources exchanged in the person-supervisor and person-coworker relationships. The proportion of time jobs involve routine tasks significantly affects job rewards only among low externals. Job rewards for personality groups derive from case load size, formal communication (with the exception of high externals), and job autonomy.

Person-organization resources significantly affect job rewards. However, the standardized regression coefficients show that these effects vary in importance across personality groups. The direct effects of formal communication, case load size, and job autonomy on job rewards shows that the positive reinforcement characteristics of exchange resources varies by personality group.

Most important to job rewards among the high internal group is case load size (−.158) followed by job autonomy (.149) and formal communication (.133). The formal communication effect is most important to job rewards among low internals (.186), followed by job autonomy (.141), and case load size (.118). The low external group values job autonomy (.166) above case load size (−.140) and formal communication (.091). Finally, case load size (−.205) and job autonomy (.203) are equally important to job rewards among high externals. Formal communication is not a significant contributor to job rewards for this group.

Resources exchanged in the person-supervisor, person-coworker, and person-client relationships have smaller effects on job rewards for the personality sub-groups than resources exchanged in the person-organization relationship. Receiving encouragement from supervisors has a marginally significant effect on rewards for low internals and low externals (p <= .10; .076, .073, respectively), and high externals (p<= .05; .151). This resource is clearly more important for externals—especially high externals. The supervisor encouragement effect on job rewards is not significant among high internals. Age-, race-, and sex-bias among supervisors has a significant effect on rewards only among high externals (P<= .10; .123).

Age-, race-, and sex-bias among coworkers does not significantly affect rewards. However, like supervisor encouragement, coworker encouragement is an important positive reinforcer. Encouragement from coworkers contributes to rewards among high internals (.107) and low externals (.086), but is not a significant reward source for low internals and high externals. Finally, belief that clients deserve HSA services increases positive reinforcement for high internals (.232), low internals (.200), low externals (.173), and high externals (.279).

Table 8. OLS Regression of Rewards (R), Costs (C), and Profit (P) on Resources for Locus of Control personality groups[a]

Exchange relationships	High Internals (N=302)			Low Internals (N=639)			Low Externals (N=591)			High Externals (N=285)		
	Rewards	Costs	Profit	Rewards	Costs	Profit	Rewards	Costs	Profit	Rewards	Costs	Profit
Employee-organization												
% routine tasks	−.008	.073	.032	.064	−.012	−.048	.080+	.088+	−.123*	.038	−.099+	.076
Size of caseload[b]	−.158*	.254*	−.231*	−.118*	.217*	−.192*	−.140*	.249*	−.227*	−.205*	.161*	−.211*
Formal communication[b]	.133*	−.024	.073	.186*	−.091*	.169*	.091*	−.091*	.102*	.036	−.082	.020
Job autonomy	.149*	.144*	.165*	.142*	−.121*	.140*	.166*	−.172*	.190*	.203*	−.280*	.270*
Employee-supervisor												
Supervisor encouragement	−.094	.004	−.052	.076+	−.027	.071+	.073+	−.020	−.058	.151*	−.015	.109+
Supervisor bias	−.054	.055	−.055	.034	−.067	−.011	.050	.023	−.011	.123+	−.009	.097
Employee-coworker												
Coworker encouragement	.107*	.066	.121*	−.020	.003	−.017	.086*	−.022	.067	−.030	−.028	−.037
Coworker bias	.077	.004	.024	.028	−.007	.014	−.023	.058	−.036	−.071	−.050[c]	−.057

Table 8. OLS Regression of Rewards (R), Costs (C), and Profit (P) on Resources for Locus of Control personality groups[a]

Exchange relationships	High Internals (N=302)			Low Internals (N=639)			Low Externals (N=591)			High Externals (N=285)		
	Rewards	Costs	Profit	Rewards	Costs	Profit	Rewards	Costs	Profit	Rewards	Costs	Profit
Employee-client												
Client deservedness	.232*	.154*	.250*	.200*	−.152*	.197*	.173*	−.227*	.214*	.279*	−.232*	.321*
Constant	3.836	7.149	−.928	4.978	6.533	−.845	1.775	7.982	−5.687	.764	11.264	−8.763
R^2	.291*	.357*	.361*	.209*	.296*	.297	.164*	.295*	.272*	.172*	.249*	.256*

a. Each equation includes 13 control variables whose coefficients are not reported here but are available from the author. These control variables are: job tenure, salary, age, sex, race, marital status (4 dummy variables), job title (3 dummy variables) and education. Standardized regression coefficients are reported.

b. Scale reverse coded for consistency—a high score reflects more of the concept measured.

c. Coefficient multiplied by 1000.

* $p <= .05$

+ $p <= .10$

Several conclusions regarding variation in the positive reinforcement characteristics that exchange resources have for internals and externals are evident from these regression results. First, each workplace relationship contains resources that are important sources of positive reinforcement for some personality groups. Resources exchanged in the person-organization relationship contribute more to rewards across personality groups than resources offered in the other exchange relationships. Second, the relative contribution of exchange resources to rewards is not consistent across personality groups. Generally, of the significant resource effects on job rewards, job autonomy is most important and formal communication is least important. In fact, the formal communication effect on rewards is only significant for three of the four personality groups.

Job Costs

The analysis of job costs reveals that exchange resources generally contribute more to positive than negative reinforcement. Like positive reinforcement, more resources exchanged in the person-organization relationship affect job costs than resources exchanged in the other relationships. Case load size and job autonomy effects on job costs are significant for each personality group. Formal communication is important among low internals and low externals, and receiving routine tasks is costly only for low and high external groups.

The size of the case load size effect on job costs does not differ significantly across the four personality groups, but case load size appears to be slightly more salient for internals compared to externals. Among resources exchanged in person-organization relationship, case load size contributes more to costs for high internals (.254), low internals (.217), and low externals (.249) than other resources. Case load size (.161) is second in importance to job autonomy (−.280) for high externals. These results indicate that receiving more cases than can be managed effectively is generally more costly for internals. For high externals, however, receiving little job autonomy is the greatest source of negative reinforcement.

The strong association between low job autonomy and job costs among high externals is shared by low externals. Lacking job autonomy is second in magnitude among person-organization resources associated with job costs for low externals (−.172), low internals (−.121), and high internals (−.144). These coefficients show that a lack of job autonomy is significantly more costly for externals than internals. This finding is surprising, given that internals tend to value job autonomy more than externals. Similarly, the formal communication effect on job costs was not anticipated. Formal communication has the same effect on job costs for low internals and low externals (–.091), but is not important among high internals and high externals. Finally, the effect of receiving routine tasks on job costs for externals is worth noting. Job costs increase for low externals who receive routine tasks in workplace exchanges (.088), while the same conditions decrease costs for high externals (p<=.10; –.099).

Resources exchanged in the person-supervisor and person-coworker relationships had no impact on job costs for any personality group. Resources exchanged in the person-client relationship did, however, affect job costs. Perceiving clients as worthy of receiving HSA services and exhibiting self-helping behaviors increases job costs for high internals (–.154), low internals (–.152), low externals (–.227), and high externals (–.232). In fact, of all the resources that contribute to job costs, this factor is second in importance for each personality group.

The data show asymmetric effects of exchange resources on job rewards and job costs across personality groups. That is, exchange resources contribute differentially to positive reinforcement and negative reinforcement. Therefore, the effects of job rewards *and* job costs on turnover must be considered simultaneously. I accomplish this by calculating a measure of net profit obtained from exchange resource by subtracting job rewards scores from job costs scores. Profit represents the net effect of the positive and negative reinforcement qualities of exchange resources, or the value employees place on exchange resources.

Profit in the Workplace

Case load size, job autonomy, and client self-helping behaviors are the only resources that have a significant effect on profit for all four personality groups. For each personality group, client deservedness is the most salient resource exchanged in the four workplace relationships. Overall, externals appear to place more value on this resource than internals, relative to other resources. The difference in the client deservedness effect on profit for high externals (.321) and low internals (.197) is significant. The client deservedness effect on profit for low externals (.227) and high internals (.250) is similar to that effect among low internals.

Job autonomy is also more important to profit among externals than other resources. The coefficients for high externals (.270) and low externals (.190) are significantly different from low internals (.140), but not high internals (.165). Case load size is the second most salient resource for high internals (–.231), low internals (–.192), and low externals (–.227); it is third in importance among the other resources for high externals (–.221). Finally, formal communication is an important source of profit for low internals (.169) and low externals (.102), and the routine tasks effect on profit is significant only among low externals.

Resources exchanged in person-supervisor and person-coworker relationships generally show little effect on job profits across personality groups. Supervisor encouragement contributes marginally to profits for low internals (p< .10; .071) and high externals (p< .10; .109). Coworker encouragement affects profit only for high internals (.121). Supervisor and coworker bias effects on profit are not significant among any of the personality groups.

Two important conclusions can be drawn from the analysis of exchange resource effects on profit. First, employees value the resources they receive in the person-organization relationship over those received in the other workplace relationships. Second, significant variation exists in the value that employees in different personality groups place on exchange resources, and in the resources that these groups find valuable. These conclusions find further support in evidence reported in Table 9 showing that exchange resource effects on rewards, costs, and profit differ for the sample when compared to internal and external groups.

The regression of rewards, costs, and profit on exchange resources for the four personality groups supports my second hypothesis and partially supports my third hypothesis. First, internals and externals perceive exchange resources differently and place different value on these resources. However, the resources valued among particular personality groups were not always as expected. Second, exchange ideology affected perceptions of exchange resources, but not as much as LOC. Third, as stated in my third hypothesis, exchange ideology is related to LOC.

Table 9. OLS Regression of Rewards, Costs, and Profit on Exchange Resources for the Total Sample[a]

Independent variables	Rewards	Costs	Profit
Resources			
% routine tasks	−.042	.022	−.054*
Size of case load	.140*	−.221*	.206*
Agency communication	−.126*	.082*	−.113*
Job autonomy	.160*	−.166*	.177*
Supervisor encouragement	−.061*	−.020	−.053*
Supervisor bias	.031	.035	.001
Coworker support	.032	−.016	.028
Coworker bias	.011	.030	−.011
Client deservedness	.200*	−.183*	.222*
R^2	.218*	.311*	.306*

a. Each equation includes 13 control variables whose coefficients are not reported here but are available from the author. These control variables are: job tenure, salary, age, sex, race, marital status (4 dummy variables), job title (3 dummy variables), LOC, and education. Standardized regression coefficient reported.

* $p <= .05$

The Odds of Quitting

According to the social exchange model of quitting developed in this paper, employee LOC interacts with work conditions to determine quitting. That is, employees tend to quit jobs that offer low profit, when comparison level is high and alternatives exist; and, the effect of profit on quitting depends on employee LOC. I test this model while controlling for variables drawn from other influential models of turnover. Table 10 shows the results of modeling quits using Price's definition of turnover; employees who quit receive a "1" and those who did not quit receive a "0" (i.e., stay, transfer, promote). Table 11 shows the results of modeling quits when employees who experienced turnover by transferring or promotion are excluded from the analysis. The coefficients in Tables 10 and 11 are the exponentiated log of the odds of quitting; they represent the multiplicative effect of the independent variables on the odds of quitting.

The coefficients in Table 10 show that occupation, sex, age and salary are the only demographic effects on quitting that reach statistical significance. When compared to social counselors, disability claims examiners (.249) and eligibility counselors (.545) tend to quit less. The gender effect shows that being female decreases the odds of quitting by more than 40 percent, when compared to males. The age effect shows that older employees quit more than their younger counterparts (1.028). Finally, a significant salary effect (1.000) indicates that the odds of quitting are about even for higher and lower salaried employees, net of other effects.

Net of other effects, integration, formal communication, and job autonomy effects are not significant (see Table 10). The opportunity effect is significant (1.270), but job satisfaction, an important determinant of quitting in most turnover research, is not. In fact, only two variables from traditional turnover models, opportunity and salary, have significant effects on quitting net of the social exchange model variables and LOC.

The data support the social exchange model of quitting. The direct profit effect is significant (.831), indicating that employees who receive low profits tend to quit more than those who receive high profits. Employees also tend to quit when they perceive easy access to an alternative employment relationship. However, comparing personal work conditions to those of other employees and the direct effect of LOC are not significant, and LOC does not interact with profit to determine the odds of quitting (when contrasted with stays, transfers and promotions). Finally, the odds of quitting are greater for employees who have a weak exchange ideology compared to employees with a high exchange ideology.

The evidence presented in Table 11 derives from the logistic regression of the odds of quitting or staying, when all other turnover is omitted from the analysis. These results differ significantly from the results in Table 10 which were obtained by estimating the same model with quitting contrasted against staying, transferring, and promoting behaviors. The improvement chi-square, over the constant only model, is substantially greater (21.788) in Table 11 than in Table 10, even though the same degrees of freedom are used in estimating both equations. Calculating Aldrich and Nelson's (1984) $R^2 = X^2/(X^2 + N)$ reveals that an additional 2% of the variation in the odds of quitting is explained when using the sample that excludes other types of turnover (Table 11). Occupation, sex, salary, and age remain the only significant demographic effects and, in fact, they are essentially identical despite the difference in the way the dependent variable is coded.

Table 10. Logistic Regression of the Odds of Quitting Versus Staying, Transferring, and Promoting[a]

Independent variables	Odds of quitting Exp(B)
Tenure in current job (in years)	.966
Job[b]	
Disability claims examiner	.249*
Eligibility counselor	.545*
Vocational rehabilitation counselor	1.206
Race (White=1)	.930
Sex (Female=1)	.578*
Age (in years)	1.028*
Salary, annual ($)	1.000*
Education	.979
Profit (overall job rewards-costs)	.831*
Comparison of negative job features to others' jobs	1.070
Ease of finding another job	1.270*
Exchange ideology	.895*
LOC	.917
Profit × LOC	1.015
Job satisfaction	.920
Job satisfaction × LOC	1.011
Job commitment	2.203*
Job commitment × LOC	.006
Constant	−2.988
Improvement chi-square (over constant only model)	172.478*
Percentage of cases correctly predicted=	88.16

a. The equation includes 10 control variables whose coefficients are not reported here but are available from the author. These control variables are: Size of case load, % of routine tasks, job autonomy, formal agency communication, supervisor support, supervisor bias, coworker support, coworker bias, client deservedness and marital status. None of these control variables are statistically significant in the equation.

b. The benchmark categories are as follows: job, social counselor.

c. Coefficient multiplied by 10.

* p <= .05

Table 11. Logistic Regression of the Odds of Quitting Versus Staying[a]

Independent variables	Odds of quitting Exp(B)
Tenure in current job (in years)	.964*
Job[b]	
Disability claims examiner	.217*
Eligibility counselor	.457*
Vocational rehabilitation counselor	1.030
Race (White=1)	.807
Sex (Female=1)	.611*
Age (in years)	1.026*
Salary, annual ($)	1.000*
Education	.979
Profit (job rewards-costs)	.796*
Comparison of negative job features to others' jobs	1.105
Ease of finding another job	1.308*
Exchange ideology	.880*
LOC	.844
Profit × LOC	1.020*
Job satisfaction	.877
Job satisfaction × LOC	1.017
Job commitment	2.087*
Job commitment × LOC	1.006
Constant	−1.541
Improvement chi-square (over constant only model)	193.788*
Percentage of cases correctly predicted=	87.18

a. The equation includes 10 control variables whose coefficients are not reported here but are available from the author. These control variables are: Size of case load, % of routine tasks, job autonomy, formal agency communication, supervisor support, supervisor bias, coworker support, coworker bias, client deservedness and marital status. None of these control variables are statistically significant in the equation.
b. The benchmark category is social counselor.
* $p <= .05$

The effects of variables that constitute the social exchange model of turnover change significantly when the odds of quitting are contrasted with staying, transferring, and promoting (Table 10), and when the odds of quitting are contrasted only with staying (Table 11). In Table 11, the profit (.796) and opportunity (1.308) effects are greater than they are in Table 10, the comparison level and LOC effects are not significant in Table 11, but the LOC × profit interaction effect (1.020) is significant. The coefficients in Table 11 show that the odds of quitting are not significantly different for internals and externals, but that profit is more relevant for internals making quitting decisions than it is for externals.

The results displayed in Table 11 support my fourth hypothesis. Employees are more likely to quit when job costs are greater than job rewards and when alternative employment opportunities exist. Moreover, the effect of the job rewards-costs difference (i.e., profit) depends on LOC. The social exchange model in Table 11 clearly shows that the effect of employee evaluations of work conditions on quitting depends on personality.

Personality effects on employee evaluations of work conditions and turnover appear more striking when quits are modeled separately for internals and externals. Table 12 presents logistic regressions of the odds of quitting for the sub-samples of internals and externals. These results are similar to those for the entire sample presented in Table 11. Low job profit and available job alternatives increase the odds of quitting only for internals. Conversely, the effects for externals show that neither profit nor the availability of job alternatives is relevant to their quit decisions. In fact, a different model altogether predicts quitting behavior among externals.

The variables that predict quitting among externals differ markedly from those that determine quits among internals. Job satisfaction has a direct effect on the odds of quitting for externals (1.175; p=.06). Job autonomy, supervisor age-, race-, and sex-bias, and client deservedness also affect quitting among externals. These results suggest that satisfaction is a determinant of turnover only among externals. Employees who feel more in control of their environment use different information about their work environment to make quitting decisions than employees with a lesser sense of personal agency. That is, employees who believe that they can influence the employment relationship evaluate contextual work factors in order to make rational decisions about quitting. On the other hand, employees who believe that work factors are fated and beyond their influence tend to make work related decisions based more on assessments of exchange resources reflected in attitudes (i.e., job satisfaction) rather than those based on rational evaluations of exchange resources (i.e., profit).

The analysis of turnover confirms my fourth hypothesis; employees tend to leave jobs that offer low profit, when alternatives exist. Moreover,

LOC interacts with the profit employees derive from work conditions to lower the effect of profit on the odds of quitting for externals, and comparison level does not affect the odds of quitting.

This analysis presents two other findings that are worth noting. First, the social exchange model of turnover receives more support in this analysis than models that use job satisfaction to explain quitting (cf., Price, 1977). Only two variables in Price's model, salary and opportunity, were significant net of the effects of variables representing the social exchange model. Second, coding the dependent variable to contrast quits with staying, transferring, and promoting, versus contrasting quits with staying, significantly affects the logistic regression results. The biggest difference occurs in the occupation effect. The most important signal, however, of the differential effects that derive from the two coding schemes is the improvement in chi-square over the constant only equations and a 2% difference in the R-square—indicating that the data fit the regression equation better when quits are modeled with other turnover excluded from the analysis.

My fifth hypothesis is not confirmed. Exchange ideology is, in fact, inversely related to quitting. Employees with a high exchange ideology have lower odds of quitting than employees with a low exchange ideology. This suggests that the relationship between personality characteristics needs further study, especially in terms of interaction effects among personality characteristics and between personality characteristics and work variables.

Summary

The evidence presented in this chapter shows that work conditions are not viewed identically by all employees. Personality plays a significant role in determining how employees perceive and evaluate work conditions. Employee evaluations of work conditions, in terms of overall job profit, are more relevant to turnover decisions for employees who have an internal LOC than they are for externals. Externals base their quitting decisions on the content of job autonomy; supervisor age-, race-, and sex-bias; and client deservedness they receive in workplace exchanges. In short, the wealth of evidence presented in this chapter provides strong support for concluding that personality interacts with work conditions to determine quitting behavior.

The general hypothesis that group characteristics affect employees' perceptions and evaluations of exchange resources, and that these characteristics affect quitting decisions will be revisited in the next chapter. Perceptions and evaluations of exchange resources and quitting are examined separately for each occupation group. This analysis will impact how the relationship between personality, work conditions, and turnover is described.

Table 12. Logistic Regression of the Odds of Quitting for Internals and Externals (EXP (B) coefficients are reported)[a]

Independent variables	Internals (N=1184)	Externals (N=440)
Tenure in current job (in years)	.971	.921
Job[b]		
Disability claims examiner	.218*	.196
Eligibility counselor	.478*	.350*
Vocational rehabilitation counselor	.847	2.385
Race (White=1)	.738	1.169
Sex (Female=1)	.677	.248*
Age (in years)	1.024	1.042*
Salary, annual ($)	1.000*	1.000*
Education	.983	.994
Manageability of caseload	1.016	1.111
Formal communication	.950	1.010
% of routine tasks	.982	1.003
Job autonomy	1.024	1.258*
Supervisor encouragement	.977	.957
Supervisor bias	1.052	1.235*
Coworker encouragement	.977	1.073+
Coworker bias	.977	1.128+
Client deservedness	1.040	.857*
Profit (job rewards-costs)	.920*	1.101
Comparison of negative job features to others' jobs	1.130	.872
Ease of finding another job	.332*	1.039
Exchange ideology	.835*	1.030
Job satisfaction	.988	1.175+
Job commitment	2.427*	1.897*
Constant	.539	−2.865
Improvement chi-square	146.310*	89.685*
Percentage of cases correctly predicted	88.05	88.64

a. Coefficients for marital status did not reach statistical significance and are not reported here.

b. The benchmark category is social counselor.

* $p <= .05$; + $p <= .10$

IV

Occupational Differences in Exchange Resources and Quitting

The analysis of work conditions, personality, and quitting in chapter three revealed that internals and externals perceive the same work conditions differently. Internals and externals also place different value on these work conditions. Moreover, the LOC effect on perceptions *and* evaluations of work conditions is important for predicting quitting behavior. Quitting among the two personality groups is explained by different models. Research on occupations and personality suggests that occupation may also determine how employees perceive and evaluate work conditions (Goffman, 1956; Kohn, 1981; Ronen and Sudan, 1984), and how these processes affect quitting behavior.

Work conditions vary across occupations and employees' perceptions and evaluations of work conditions affect quitting decisions. Each of the four occupations in this study has a distinct configuration of work conditions. An analysis of the variation in perceptions and evaluations of work conditions across occupations is needed to test the generalizability of work condition effects on quitting. Such information will help to identify which work conditions are universal determinants of quitting and which are only significant for particular occupational groups. This analysis will inform about the appropriate operationalization of work conditions for specific populations under investigation.

Occupational Differences in Work Conditions

The four occupations in this study offer employees varying amounts of job autonomy, task routinization, formal communication, case load size, and supervisor, coworker and client interaction. This variation derives, in part, from differences in work conditions observed in standard job descriptions and, in part, from employees' perceptions of these work conditions. The following description of the institutional differences in occupations that structure resource allocation and resource exchanges comes from interpreting official HSA Department of Personnel job descriptions and personal interviews with HSA administrators about the work context and context of each occupation.

Eligibility counselors function as the agency's "front door." They conduct face-to-face interviews with applicants for HSA services and verify this information to determine applicant eligibility for services. Eligibility counselors also complete and maintain a budget worksheet for each client and a report on client's financial and personal status.

Social counselors provide services to adults, children, and clients who are physically or mentally ill, disabled, aged, abused and/or neglected. After interviewing clients and identifying their needs, social counselors help clients and their family members adjust to complex social, health, emotional, and economic problems. Social counselors work closely with other social service agencies to coordinate services, and prepare social studies, case histories, and evaluations concerning information they acquire and the services they render. In addition, social counselors provide services to other social services programs (e.g., licensing care facilities, work incentive, adoption, foster care). Vocational rehabilitation counselors generally perform similar functions in their work with handicapped persons.

Disability claims examiners determine claimants' eligibility for social security disability benefits. In order to make this determination, disability claims examiners analyze medical and vocational data, and consult with claimants and medical professionals to determine the extent and duration of disabilities and claimants' ability to work. They also refer clients to various training and evaluation programs designed to prepare clients for employment and report weekly on clients' progress. Disability claims examiners work closely with clients, but function largely independent of direct supervision and work teams.

Several functions in each occupation are similar: assessing client needs and eligibility for HSA services, and administering these services or making referrals to the appropriate agencies. These functions require that employees exchange their labor for work conditions that are similar across occupations. The four occupations differ with respect to their level of job autonomy, client intimacy, supervision, and opportunity for coworker interaction.

According to the official job descriptions and comments of personnel administrators, the major occupational differences in work conditions exist between eligibility counselors and the other three occupations. Social counselors, vocational rehabilitation counselors, and disability claims examiners are less dissimilar.

Eligibility counselors have the least amount of flexibility in performing their jobs. They work from a stationary office space, are members of work groups, and have standard protocols for determining client eligibility for HSA services. Eligibility counselors use much less personal judgment in performing their job tasks than the other occupations. The other occupations follow procedure, but they also make subjective decisions when assessing client needs and coordinating resources from HSA and other agencies (this is particularly true of social and vocational rehabilitation counselors).

The assessment and coordination roles performed by social counselors, vocational rehabilitation counselors, and disability claims examiners occur in an environment of less supervision and coworker interaction than is the case for eligibility counselors. Coordinating resources from departments within HSA and other agencies requires that members of these occupations extend their work places beyond the confines of HSA buildings. Social counselors, in particular, perform much of their assessment and inspecting of businesses that deliver human services (e.g., day care centers) in clients' homes or at business locations. These occupational work conditions restrict the level of supervision that can occur for social counselors, vocational rehabilitation counselors, and disability claims examiners, and the opportunities for them to interact with coworkers.

The intake and administrative duties that eligibility counselors perform are clearly more routine and repetitious than the other occupations. Eligibility counselors also interact with more applicants and clients than the other occupations—albeit on a more superficial level. The other occupations have more intimate contact with clients by virtue of their roles as service coordinators and case managers (social counselors and vocational rehabilitation counselors have the most intimate client contact).

Differences in the four occupations described above affect employees' opportunity to receive different exchange resources. The major institutional differences exist between the work conditions of eligibility counselors when compared to the other occupations. I now examine whether occupational groups selectively perceive and evaluate their respective work conditions.

Occupation and Exchange Resources

Table 13 presents results of t-tests comparing means on exchange resources for each occupation. These results show that the most consistent perceptual differences in exchange resources occur between eligibility counselors and the other occupations. Occupational differences in perceived work conditions are particularly evident with respect to resources exchanged in the person-organization exchange relationship.

Disability claims examiners perceive more formal communication than eligibility, vocational rehabilitation, and social counselors; while social counselors say they receive more of this resource than vocational rehabilitation counselors. Disability claims examiners also perceive fewer routine tasks than eligibility counselors, but more than vocational rehabilitation and social counselors. Disability claims examiners and vocational rehabilitation counselors perceive a greater case load size than eligibility and social counselors. Finally, disability claims examiners and eligibility counselors score lower on the job autonomy scale than vocational rehabilitation and social counselors.

Fewer significant occupational differences exist in perceptions of resources exchanged in the person-supervisor, person-coworker, and person-client relationships. Disability claims examiners say that their supervisors offer more encouragement compared to eligibility and social counselors. Disability claims examiners, compared to vocational rehabilitation counselors, tend to disagree that clients deserve HSA services. In fact, vocational rehabilitation counselors score higher on the client deservedness scale than each of the other occupations, while social counselors score higher than eligibility counselors. Eligibility counselors, who have the least amount of intimate client contact, register the lowest client deservedness score.

The results of OLS regression analysis performed on occupational subgroups support findings reported in Table 13 that show how mean scores on perceptions of exchange resources differ across occupations. Table 14 shows metric regression coefficients for the occupation dummy variable effect on perceptions of exchange resources. Regression equations were estimated for every configuration of the occupation dummy variables. These equations produced coefficients for occupation effects that can be compared from occupation to occupation. Each coefficient represents the effect of being in the occupational category in the column compared to being in the occupational category on the row. That is, the occupation on the row is the benchmark category.

Table 13. T-tests of the Difference Between Means on Exchange Resources for Disability Claims Examiners (1), Eligibility Counselors (2), Social Counselors (3), and Vocational Rehabilitation Counselors (4)[a]

Exchange resources		Occupation			
		1	2	3	4
		DCE	EC	SC	VRC
Manageability of case load	1.	4.4			
	2.	*	3.7		
	3.	*	ns	3.8	
	4.	ns	*	ns	4.8
Formal communication	1.	14.3			
	2.	*	12.6		
	3.	*	ns	12.7	
	4.	*	ns	*	12.3
% of routine tasks	1.	10.8			
	2.	*	11.7		
	3.	*	*	8.9	
	4.	*	*	ns	9.2
Job autonomy	1.	6.6			
	2.	ns	7.0		
	3.	*	*	7.6	
	4.	*	*	ns	7.7
Supervisor encouragement	1.	22.8			
	2.	*	21.7		
	3.	*	ns	21.5	
	4.	ns	ns	ns	22.1
Client deservedness	1.	.20			
	2.	ns	−.43		
	3.	ns	*	.24	
	4.	*	*	ns	1.94

a. Mean scores on exchange resources are listed for each occupation on the diagonals of the matrices. An "*" or "ns" below the diagonal represents the significance level of the difference in mean scores for two occupations. The scores for Supervisor and Coworker age-, race-, and sex-bias and for Coworker encouragement do not differ significantly across occupation and are not reported here.

* $p \leq .05$

ns   p is not significant

Table 14. Metric Regression Coefficients for Occupational Dummy Variables from OLS Regressions of Exchange Resources on Disability Claims Examiners (1), Eligibility Counselors (2), Social Counselors (3), and Vocational Rehabilitation Counselors (4)[a]

Exchange resources	Row occupation		Column occupation		
			DCE (1)	(2)	(3)
Manageability of case load	EC	(2)	−.586*		
	SC	(3)	−.593*	−.006	
	VRC	(4)	.480	1.006*	1.072*
Formal communication	EC	(2)	.822*		
	SC	(3)	.918*	.096	
	VRC	(4)	1.305	.483+	.388
% of routine tasks	EC	(2)	−.930*		
	SC	(3)	1.826*	2.755*	
	VRC	(4)	1.755*	2.684*	−.071
Job autonomy	EC	(2)	−.137		
	SC	(3)	−.871*	−.733*	
	VRC	(4)	−1.021*	−.885*	−.151
Supervisor encouragement	EC	(2)	.984*		
	SC	(3)	1.323*	.339+	
	VRC	(4)	.649	−.335	−.674+
Client deservedness	EC	(2)	.809		
	SC	(3)	−.012	−.820*	
	VRC	(4)	−1.376+	−2.185*	−1.365*

a. The occupation effects were derived by estimating four regression equations that each contained a different occupation as the benchmark category. The coefficients represent the effect of being n the occupation on the column compared to the occupation on the row (the missing category). The equations that produced these coefficients included 11 variables whose coefficients are not reported here but are available from the author. The coefficients for Coworker age-, race-, and sex-bias and Coworker encouragement do not differ significantly across occupation and are not reported here.

* $p \leq .05$

+ $p \leq .10$

Disability claims examiners describe their case loads as more manageable compared to eligibility and social counselors (−.586 and −.593, respectively), but less manageable than vocational rehabilitation examiners (.480). Disability claims examiners also report having less job autonomy than vocational rehabilitation and social counselors (−1.021 and −.871, respectively); having more routine tasks than social (1.826) and vocational rehabilitation (1.755) counselors, but fewer than eligibility counselors (−.930); and receiving less formal communication than eligibility (.822), social (.918), and vocational rehabilitation (1.305) counselors. Finally, disability claims examiners are more likely than vocational rehabilitation counselors to characterize their clients as not deserving HSA services (−1.376, p<=.10), and their supervisors as more encouraging than those of eligibility (.984) and social (1.323) counselors.

Eligibility counselors receive more manageable case loads than vocational rehabilitation counselors (1.006), less job autonomy than social (−.733) and vocational rehabilitation (−.885) counselors, more routine tasks than social (2.755) and vocational rehabilitation (2.684) counselors, and more formal communication than vocational rehabilitation counselors. Eligibility counselors also say their supervisors are more encouraging compared to social counselors (.339), and that their clients are less deserving of HSA services compared to social (−.820) and vocational rehabilitation (−2.185) counselors.

Social counselors report having a more manageable case load and less supervisor encouragement than vocational rehabilitation counselors report having (1.072 and −.674, respectively), and score lower on the client deservedness scale than vocational rehabilitation counselors (−1.365).

Occupational differences in perceptions of exchange resources observed in Tables 13 and 14 support the argument that occupation determines the availability of exchange resources. In fact, the multivariate analysis (Table 14) actually revealed meaningful occupational differences in perceptions of exchange resources that were not indicated by comparing means across occupations. Eligibility counselors perceive the most task routinization while social counselors report the least. Social and vocational rehabilitation counselors report the most job autonomy while disability claims examiners and eligibility counselors perceive the least. Eligibility and social counselors have the most manageable case loads while disability claims examiners and vocational rehabilitation counselors have the least manageable case loads. Formal communication is greatest for disability claims examiners and least for vocational rehabilitation counselors. Supervisor encouragement is greatest for disability claims examiners and vocational rehabilitation counselors. Finally, eligibility counselors and claims examiners perceive clients as undeserving of HSA services.

Analysis of HSA job descriptions and employees' perceptions of these work conditions across occupations provides compelling evidence that occupational work conditions differ significantly and are perceived as such by occupation members. This observation and the findings reported in chapter three showing significant LOC effects on perceptions of work conditions support the view that occupation *and* personality affect perceptions of work conditions. The reinforcement qualities of these work conditions are examined for each occupation in the next section.

Occupational Differences in Rewards, Costs and Profit

Identifying how employees perceive work conditions is a necessary but insufficient criterion for understanding quitting behavior. It is also important to identify how employees evaluate their work conditions. In this study, employees' evaluations of work conditions are identified by analyzing work condition effects on job rewards, job costs, and profit. I estimate regression equations that control demographic variables, work attitudes, and personality to examine these effects for each occupation. The standardized regression coefficients generated in this analysis will reveal if significant differences exist in the positive, negative, and absolute reinforcement that members of different occupations receive from exchange resources. Unfortunately, because twenty degrees of freedom are required to estimate these equations, the sample of disability claims examiners (N=69) must be omitted from this analysis. The sample of vocational rehabilitation counselors is also relatively small (N=126) for these equations. Vocational rehabilitation counselors will be included in the analysis; however, caution must be exercised in interpreting the results for these employees.

The results of the OLS regression of rewards, costs, and profit on exchange resources, LOC, and demographic variables appear in Table 15. Given the exploratory nature of these analyses, effects that have a P-value of .05 or below will be discussed in detail, but all effects significant at P<=.10 will be presented. Generally, the regression analysis reveals significant occupational differences in the positive (i.e., rewards) and negative (i.e., costs) reinforcement qualities of exchange resources, and in the absolute value (i.e., profit) that vocational rehabilitation counselors, social counselors, and eligibility counselors attribute to these resources.

Table 15. OLS Regression of Rewards, Costs, and Profit on Exchange Resources for Occupation Subgroups[a]

Exchange resources	Vocational Rehabilitation Counselors			Social Counselors			Eligibility Counselors		
	Rewards	Costs	Profit	Rewards	Costs	Profit	Rewards	Costs	Profit
Employee-organization									
% routine tasks	.038	.010	−.040	.049	−.001	−.047	−.030	.041	−.060*
Size of caseload[b]	−.037	.278*	−.178*	−.145*	.273*	−.221*	−.138*	.173*	−.186*
Formal communication[b]	.088	−.112	.122	.114*	−.017	.076*	.163*	−.143*	.156*
Job autonomy	.271*	−.194*	.280*	.190*	−.165*	.186*	.121*	−.155*	.145*
Employee-supervisor									
Supervisor encouragement	.100	−.078	.136	.061	−.018	.058	.058+	−.029	.053*
Supervisor bias	.184*	.062	.104	.021	.018	.024	.053	.041	.001
Employee-coworker									
Coworker encouragement	.000	−.019	−.033	−.024	−.007	.001	.068*	−.013	.049+
Coworker bias	.023	.132	−.111	−.041	.055	.000	−.019	.011	−.016
Employee-client									
Client deservedness	.126	−.103	.114	.192*	−.188*	.209*	.217*	−.201*	.251*
R^2	.137*	.210*	.230*	.181*	.252*	.242*	.230*	.209*	.288*

a. Each equation includes 11 control variables whose coefficients are not reported here but are available from the author. These variables are: job tenure, salary, age, sex, race, marital status (4 dummy variables), locus of control and education. Standardized regression coefficients are reported.

b. Scale reverse coded for consistency—a high score reflects more of the concept measured.

* $p <= .05$; + $p <= .10$

Vocational rehabilitation counselors receive reinforcement from three exchange resources. Net of other effects in the equation, greater job autonomy and supervisor bias increase job rewards (.271; 184, p<.05, respectively). Having greater job autonomy also decreases job costs among vocational rehabilitation counselors (−.194), however, job autonomy affects job rewards more than job costs. Finally, job costs increase with greater case load size (.278), and the case load size effect is 30% larger than the job autonomy effect.

When the overall profit that vocational rehabilitation counselors receive from workplace exchange resources is considered, the data show that only job autonomy and case load size hold significant value for these employees. Each unit increase in job autonomy increases job profit by .280 standard deviations. The standardized case load size effect is .178. Clearly, among the resources examined here vocational rehabilitation counselors value job autonomy the most.

The sources of positive and negative reinforcement and the exchange resources that social and eligibility counselors value come more from workplace exchange relationships than is the case for vocational rehabilitation counselors. But even among social and eligibility counselors, resources produce different reinforcement effects and overall value. Job rewards for social counselors grow as perceptions that clients deserve HSA services (.192), job autonomy, formal communication (.114), and the manageability of case loads (−.145) increase. Job costs increase for social counselors with increases in case loads (.273), the perception that clients deserve HSA services (−.188), and job autonomy (−.165). The formal communication effect on job costs, however, is not significant.

The job autonomy, case load size, and client deservedness effects are significant predictors of costs and rewards among social counselors, but their size and relative importance is not uniform. Client deservedness is the most important effect on job rewards and the second most important effect on job costs. Case load size is the most important effect on job costs, but ranks third among the resources contributing to job rewards. The second most important resource effect on job rewards is job autonomy but it ranks last among the factors affecting job costs.

In terms of overall profit, only resources exchanged with the organization and clients have significant value for social counselors. The most valuable resource for social counselors is receiving a manageable case load; net of over effects, profit decreases by .221 for every unit increase in case load size. Having clients that one considers deserving of HSA services is a close second in terms of resource value for social counselors (.209), followed by job autonomy (.186) and formal communication (.076).

Eligibility counselors receive positive and negative reinforcement from more resources than the other occupations. Job rewards increase for eligibility counselors as perceptions that their clients deserve HSA services (.217), formal communication (.163), and job autonomy (.121) increase. Job rewards also increase as case load size decreases (–.138). In addition, eligibility counselors are the only group for which exchanges with supervisors and coworkers have a significant effect on job rewards. Job rewards increase for this occupation as supervisor and coworker encouragement increase (.054 and .068, respectively).

Supervisor and coworker encouragement effects on job costs are not significant, suggesting that supervisor and coworker encouragement may be a source of satisfaction but not dissatisfaction. Each of the other resources that affect job rewards also have some effect on job costs, although the importance of the resource effects to positive and negative reinforcement varies. Client deservedness is the most important resource to job costs (–.201) followed by case load size (.173), job autonomy (–.155), and formal communication (–.143).

The analysis of job profit for eligibility counselors shows that each workplace relationship offers resources valued by these employees. Each resource in the person-organization relationship contributes to overall job profit. Case load size holds the most value among resources exchanged between these exchange partners (–.186) followed by formal communication (.156), job autonomy (.145), and routine tasks (–.068). The value attached to the routine task effect is surprising given that this resource did not effect the components of value, job rewards and job costs, individually. This underscores the importance of considering the positive and negative reinforcement qualities of work conditions, rather than only examining the positive affective response measured in the job satisfaction construct. The most valuable resource of all is a clientele that eligibility counselors feel deserves HSA services (.251) followed by the person-organization resources just described and supervisor and coworker encouragement (.053 and .049, respectively).

Only resources in the person-organization exchange relationship affect positive and negative job reinforcement and have significant value for each occupation. Having a manageable case load is a positive reinforcer for each occupation except vocational rehabilitation counselors. Moreover, even for the occupations for which the case load size effect on job rewards is significant the effect varies across occupations. The size of this effect is similar for social and eligibility counselors, and for both occupations the effect is the third most important resource to job rewards.

Having a case load that one perceives as unmanageable is the most important negative reinforcer for each occupation, but significant differences occur in the magnitude of the effect across occupations. The case load size effect on job costs is similar for vocational rehabilitation and social counselors, and the effect is larger for both groups than it is for eligibility counselors. The size difference in the effect of case load size on job costs for these three occupations is significant (using a t-test of metric regression coefficients). Finally, the effect of case load size on overall job profit indicates that it is the most valuable resource for social counselors, and the second most valuable resource for vocational rehabilitation and eligibility counselors.

Job autonomy is the second most consistent contributor to reinforcement and profit in the workplace. In fact, job autonomy increases job rewards and decreases job costs for each occupation. It is the most important resource to job rewards for vocational rehabilitation counselors, although this effect is larger for social counselors and significantly so for eligibility counselors. The job autonomy effect on job costs is equivalent for all occupations.

Job autonomy contributes more than the other exchange resources to the overall profit that vocational rehabilitation counselors receive from their employment relationship. It is the third most valuable exchange resource for social and eligibility counselors.

As reinforcers, formal communication and routine tasks are not as important as case load size and job autonomy. The formal communication effect on job rewards is significant for social and eligibility counselors, and there is little difference in the magnitude of these effects across occupations. However, formal communication is the least important among all resources contributing to job rewards for social counselors; it is the second most important effect on rewards for eligibility counselors. Furthermore, eligibility counselor is the only occupation that views the absence of formal communication as a job cost, and formal communication has the least important effect on job cost for these employees. Finally, formal communication is least important among all the resources that social and eligibility counselors value.

The routine task effect is among the least valued resources of all. It contains no significant positive or negative reinforcement for any occupation. However, the routine task effect does contribute to overall profit for eligibility counselors. This suggests that reliance on a uni-dimensional measure of reinforcement (i.e., costs , rewards, or job satisfaction) is less appropriate for assessing how employees evaluate exchange resources than a multidimensional measure like profit. The client deservedness effect on job rewards, costs, and profit is significant for social counselors and eligibility counselors. It is the most important positive reinforcement for both occupations, the most important negative reinforcement for eligibility counselors, and the second most important effect on costs for social counselors. In fact, eligibility counselors value client deservedness above all other resources, while it is the second most valuable resource for social counselors.

Three resources exchanged between employees, supervisors, and coworkers contain value and are reinforcers for vocational rehabilitation and eligibility counselors. Supervisor and coworker encouragement positively reinforce the work experience for eligibility counselors, and both are valuable resources to these employees, although they are the least valuable of all resources for eligibility counselors.

Occupations perform diverse functions within organizations. These functions structure work conditions and provide positive and negative reinforcement and overall value for occupation members. Resources in the person-organization relationship are the most important to occupation member's evaluation of work conditions. Of these, case load size and job autonomy have the most generalizable effects on such evaluations across occupations, while other resource effects vary across occupations. In short, this analysis demonstrates that the reinforcement qualities of exchange resources and the value they hold for employees differs systematically across occupations.

Occupational Differences in Quitting

The distribution of quits across occupations is presented in Table 16. Social counselors and eligibility counselors account for fifty-one percent and thirty-nine percent of all quits, respectively. Vocational rehabilitation counselors account for only eight percent of the quits and disability claims examiners account for only two percent of all quits. More important to this analysis is the proportion of each occupation that quits. Social counselors and vocational rehabilitation counselors quit the most, seventeen percent and thirteen percent, respectively; the proportions of eligibility counselors and disability claims examiners who quit is about half of that, 9 percent and 7 percent, respectively. It is important to determine if similar work conditions determine quitting across occupations, or if the particular configuration of work conditions across occupations results in a different model of quitting for these groups. Unfortunately, the number of quits among disability claims examiners and vocational rehabilitation counselors is too few to include in the following analysis of quits.

Disability claims examiners and vocational rehabilitation counselors are excluded from the multivariate analysis of quits. The degrees of freedom required to model quits are too great for the number of quits that occur in these occupations and in many cases insufficient variation exists in variables used in the regression models. Equations for these occupations could be modeled with fewer controls, but the results would not be comparable to the models for social and eligibility counselors. Vocational rehabilitation counselors and social counselors have relatively similar levels of supervision, job autonomy, case loads, and client and coworker contact. Social counselors and eligibility counselors have the greatest contrast in work conditions. In fact, the exchange resources available to these occupations approximate those described in Stinchcombe's (1979) distinction between real and subordinate professionals. Therefore, the following analysis of occupational differences in quitting will include eligibility and social counselors.

Table 16. Distribution of Quits by Occupation

Occupation (n)	Quits n (%)	Group %
Disability claims examiners (70)	5 (02)	7
Eligibility counselors (984)	84 (39)	9
Social counselors (637)	108 (51)	17
Vocational rehab. counselors (127)	17 (08)	13

Table 17 presents the logistic regression of quits for eligibility and social counselors. The coefficients in the Table are the exponentiated log of the odds of quitting. They represent the multiplicative effect of the independent variables on the odds of quitting compared to staying in the job. A coefficient of 1 indicates no effect on the odds of quitting, while effects greater than 1 increase the odds of quitting and effects less than 1 decrease the odds of quitting. The odds of a social counselor quitting are determined by job tenure, salary, profit, alternative job opportunity, exchange ideology, LOC, and the LOC × profit interaction. The odds of quitting for eligibility counselors is explained by a different model.

The odds of quitting for eligibility counselors increase with age (1.043) and the ease with which these employees could find another job (1.237, p <=.10). The turnover models reviewed in chapter one show that these effects are consistent with the neoclassical economic model of quitting, which argues that individuals work for economic gain, and they will change jobs to maximize economic profit.

Table 17 also shows, by contrast, that the effects contributing to quitting among social counselors are consistent with the social exchange model of turnover. Social counselors tend to quit when profit is low (.768, p <=.10) and when alternative employment relationships are available. The direct LOC effect is significant (.740) as is the LOC × profit interaction effect (1.029). Social counselors who have an external LOC tend to leave their jobs less often than their internal counterparts. The LOC × profit interaction term indicates that profit is more relevant for internally-oriented social counselors. Finally, the exchange ideology effect is also significant (.833)—indicating that social counselors who have a high exchange ideology have lower odds of quitting than lower exchange-oriented social counselors. This finding contradicts my fifth hypothesis and previous research (Rusbult, 1980).

The analysis of quits in Table 17 shows that eligibility counselors and social counselors quit for different reasons. The determinants of quitting among eligibility counselors are consistent with the neoclassical economic view of quitting, while quitting among social counselors is explained by the social exchange model developed in this book. Moreover, social counselors quit for the same reasons as the average individual in the study population, and the LOC × profit interaction term has the same effect within this occupation as it has among employees in general. However, only among social counselors does LOC exert a direct effect on quitting.

The comparison of factors that affect the odds of quitting for social counselors and eligibility counselors reveals that work conditions are less important for eligibility counselors. Two observations support this view. First, the regression coefficients in Table 15 show that profit is a function of work conditions. Second, the coefficients in Table 17 show that the effect of profit on the odds of quitting is significant for social counselors but not eligibility counselors.

Table 17. Logistic Regression of the Odds of Quitting for Eligibility and Social Counselors (EXP (B) coefficients are reported)

Independent variables	Eligibility (N=876)	Social (N=499)
Tenure in current job (in years)	.970	.936+
Race (White=1)	1.093	.635
Sex (Female=1)	.712	.586
Age (in years)	1.043*	1.020
Salary, annual ($)	1.000*	1.000*
Education	1.085	1.071
Marital status[c]		
Single	1.483	1.281
Divorced	.723	.500
Widowed	.696	—[c]
Separated	—[c]	.461+
Profit (job rewards-costs)	.821	.768+
Comparison of negative job features to others' jobs	.949	1.112
Ease of finding another job	1.237+	1.415*
Exchange ideology	.945	.833*
LOC	.922	.740+
Profit × LOC	1.009	1.029*
Job satisfaction	.911	.884
Job satisfaction × LOC	1.006	1.028
Job commitment	1.570	2.061
Job commitment × LOC	1.006	1.029
Constant	−8.196	−6.183
Improvement chi-square	157.361*	119.711*
Percentage of cases correctly predicted=	90.55	81.56

a. The equations include 9 control variables whose coefficients are not reported here but are available from the author. These control variables are: size of case load, % of routine tasks, job autonomy, formal communication, supervisor support, supervisor bias, coworker support, coworker bias, client deservedness. None of these control variables is statistically significant.
b. The benchmark category for marital status is married.
c. Coefficient could not be computed because there are not enough cases in this category.
* p <= .05
+ p <= .10

Summary

This analysis of exchange resources and quits reveals several important occupational differences in turnover among eligibility and social counselors. First, occupations have available to them different kinds and amounts of resources for exchange and persons in the four occupations studied here perceive these differences in ways fairly consistent to how they are articulated in official HSA job descriptions. The major perceptual differences occur between eligibility counselors and the other occupations. However, resources available to social and eligibility counselors vary the most according to the objective information. When employees' perceptions of job autonomy, formal communication, task routinization, case loads, and supervisor, coworker, and client relations were compared, the results indicate that eligibility counselors have more routine tasks, less autonomy, more supervisor interaction (in this case supportive) than social counselors. Eligibility counselors also tend to hold more negative views of their clients than social counselors. Perhaps this is due to the different level of client contact that the two occupations enjoy.

Second, the contributions that exchange resources make to positive and negative reinforcements differ for the four occupations, and the occupations' incumbents appear to value different resources. Client attitudes and behaviors are important to social counselors and eligibility counselors, but not to disability claims examiners and vocational rehabilitation counselors. Interactions with supervisors and coworkers primarily provide reinforcement and value to eligibility counselors, and to a lessor extent vocational rehabilitation counselors. Routine tasks, case loads, formal communication, and job autonomy show differential effects on reinforcements and are valued to varying degrees across occupations. Finally, there are more significant differences in the work condition effects on rewards and costs across occupations than there are in work condition effects on profit—indicating that the profit variable is more generalizable across occupations.

Third, occupation members quit for different reasons. Eligibility counselors quit when their salaries are low and when alternative jobs are available. Social counselors quit when job profit is low and when alternatives are easy to find. Social counselors who have an internal LOC quit more than their external counterparts, and profit is more relevant to internals than externals.

Occupation makes a difference for understanding how employees make quit decisions (Kohn, 1982), but not only because they shape values and norms. Occupations also structure person-workplace exchange relationships. As this research shows, occupations determine the content of resources exchanged between employees and other organizational actors. The particular resources available to occupation members affect their quitting decision indirectly through the amount of job profit they obtain. Profit significantly affects quitting for social counselors, but not for eligibility counselors.

Evidence presented in this chapter shows that the appropriate model for analyzing quits depends on the employees being examined, and their particular work conditions. Employees in occupations that offer routine tasks, low job autonomy, and high supervision (e.g., subordinate professionals and blue collar employees) quit because they believe that an employment relationship with a different employer would offer them better economic returns in exchange for their labor, skills, and talents. Work conditions did not influence quit decisions for these employees. The best model of quitting among this population is an economic model such as that proposed by March and Simon (1958). These authors argue that turnover is a function of pay and alternative job opportunities. These analyses show that this model works for the employees just described, but not the other types of employees in this sample.

Professionals and employees whose work conditions are characterized by low supervision, high job autonomy, and intimate contact with clients or customers base their quit decisions on rational evaluations of their work conditions, alternative job opportunities, and salary; and, personality interacts with their evaluation of work conditions. Moreover, LOC has a direct effect on quitting for this type of employee. The model required to predict quitting among these employees is the social exchange model of quitting developed above.

V

Discussion and Conclusions

Previous research on quitting argues that employees base their quitting decisions on work conditions, economic conditions, and personal characteristics. Important sociological, economic, and psychological models of turnover describe how these factors affect quitting. First, work conditions affect quitting indirectly by determining a worker's job satisfaction. Second, economic conditions affect the availability of alternative jobs. Third, personal characteristics identify characteristics of groups that exhibit different inclinations to quit. Most of the effort to explain turnover has been directed at identifying the relationship between work conditions, job satisfaction, and turnover. This work assumes that work conditions have a uniform effect on turnover. The evidence presented above shows that this assumption is false, and that a modified social exchange model explains quitting better than previous research.

Personality determines how employees perceive and evaluate work conditions, and how these perceptions and valuations affect quitting. These findings improve our understanding of how employees perceive and evaluate the resources they receive in the workplace, and how these valuations interact with personality to determine quitting. In this chapter I review the evidence of personality and occupation effects on quitting and discuss its implications for previous and future research on quitting.

Perceptions of Work Conditions

The employment relationship consists of employees who exchange their labor, skills, and talents with employers for work conditions and economic rewards. Work conditions are embodied in several exchange relationships involving the employee and the organization, supervisors, coworkers, and clients. This research presents evidence showing that the resources (i.e., work conditions) that employees receive in the four exchange relationships are perceived differently by segments of the HSA workforce depending on personality type (i.e., internals and externals) and occupation (i.e., eligibility counselors, social counselors, vocational rehabilitation counselors, and disability claims examiners). This finding has important implications for interpreting past research as well as the future discourse on work conditions and their turnover consequences.

Three of the most cited works on turnover either ignore personality or acknowledge it only in passing. Price (1977) and March and Simon (1958) ignore personality in their examination of work conditions, yet these authors find that work conditions determine workers' job satisfaction. Mobley (1982:129) acknowledges the need to consider personality, but only in vague terms. He assumes that personality affects "job related perceptions," but the model of turnover he presents is descriptive rather than predictive. March and Simon, Price, and Mobley conceptualize work conditions in a manner not supported by the findings presented in this study.

The analysis of personality and occupation effects on perceiving and evaluating work conditions is important for understanding which work conditions are relevant to different employees. Therefore, personality and occupation variables serve an important function in turnover research. These variables focus measures of work conditions into perceptions and valuations that have uniform meaning within the relevant groups of employees. Without such focus, as is the case in previous research, the validity of measures of employees' perceptions and valuations of work conditions is questionable. This argument suggests that the effects of such measures on quitting presented in past research are misleading. Two analyses in this study revealed that work conditions are not perceived the same by all employees. The analyses presented in Tables 7 and 14 show that internals and externals and employees in different occupations do not perceive work conditions in the same way.

Internals perceive more job autonomy, communication about issues related to doing their jobs, and supportive relations with supervisors and coworkers than externals. Internals are also more tolerant of their clients and more likely to perceive their clients as deserving of HSA services. According to LOC theory, these differences are a function of internals' tendency to exert more control in the workplace, believe that their actions determine work outcomes, and engage in interpersonal relations. On the other hand, because externals do not view their actions as contributing to work outcomes as internals do, they tend to perceive that their tasks are more routine and that their case loads are larger than internals. Externals also have more negative interpersonal relations with supervisors and clients. These findings support my first hypothesis and help to explain the modest effects of variables representing worker affective responses to work conditions, like job satisfaction, on quitting derived in previous research (Mobley et al., 1979).

The occupational variation in perceptions of work conditions reflects different exposure that occupation members have to work conditions. The kinds of work conditions that occupation members have access to differed most for eligibility counselors when compared to the other occupations. Eligibility counselors perform more routine tasks in their client intake and needs assessment role. They also work in a stationary office space that is in close proximity to supervisors and coworkers. Finally, eligibility counselors see more clients than the other occupations, but the contact between clients and eligibility counselors is less intimate than the contact between clients and the other occupations. These findings suggest that turnover researchers need to be aware of objective differences in the work conditions of employees in their study population. Workers who perform different functions within organizations may have access to different types and amounts of work conditions.

Eligibility counselors tend to perceive heavier case loads, more formal communication concerning how they should perform their jobs, routine job tasks, supervisor support and bias, and less job autonomy than the other occupations. Eligibility counselors also tend to be less tolerant of HSA clients than the other occupations. These differences are consistent with official HSA job descriptions.

Since the presence of work conditions is an objective and a subjective fact of the employment relationship, it is necessary to examine employees separately when they differ on characteristics that have a significant effect on predictor variables. As this analysis indicates, it is not enough to enter personality and occupation variables in regression equations as controls. Work conditions did not have a uniform effect on profit for personality and occupation members. This was not apparent in the equation that contained all employees and controlled on LOC and occupation. Research that ignores these important group differences will similarly distort the effects of important determinants of behavior. In this study, the distortion appeared as a smaller coefficient representing the effect of profit on quitting, and in a change in the sign of the coefficient representing the effect of alternative job opportunity on quitting.

The difference observed in internals' and externals' perceptions of work conditions largely mirrors the differences in intrinsic and extrinsic work conditions (Herzberg, 1974). Occupation differences appear to be more a function of the availability of work conditions across occupations as described in official job descriptions. However, even within occupations the personality effect aligns perceptions of work conditions into intrinsic and extrinsic categories.

Employees who attribute life experiences to forces beyond their control (i.e., externals) perceive more intrinsic work conditions. It is important to note that intrinsic work conditions like the manageability of caseloads and task routinization are precisely those that are generally outside the control of workers. On the other hand, employees who have experienced a stronger sense of personal agency in life events perceive more extrinsic job resources like coworker and supervisor support. These findings show a fit between worker personality and work conditions (Kohn, 1982). They also suggest that externals and internals tend to selectively perceive resources that match their personality type.

The analysis of work conditions for personality and occupation groups suggests that internals, externals, and occupation members live in separate worlds within the same workplace. The analysis also shows that examining work conditions without considering personality and occupation effects on perceptions of work conditions will lead to a misinterpretation of the effects of work conditions on behavioral outcomes. Specifically, the effect of work conditions on quitting for a sample which is not differentiated by LOC or occupation represents an effect that is averaged across these groups. These findings are strong support for my first hypothesis which states that internals and externals perceive the same work conditions differently. Moreover, the occupational analysis shows that this hypothesis can be expanded to include occupation.

Since only a limited list of work conditions was examined in this study, the personality effect on other work conditions needs further study. In the absence of theoretical direction or empirical observation, it is not possible to predict this relationship with certainty. However, the analysis of personality effects on perceptions of the work conditions examined here suggests that LOC theory provides a useful foundation for developing further hypotheses regarding the relationship between personality and work conditions not examined here (Rotter, 1966). Future research should reexamine the previous theoretical and empirical work on the relationship between work conditions, job satisfaction, and turnover to verify those findings in light of the evidence of the important personality and occupation effects presented in this study.

Theorists have suggested the importance of perception in determining behavior (Thomas, 1978; Goffman, 1959). According to Thomas, "if men define situations as real, they are real in their consequences." The present study is the first to rigorously apply this principle in turnover research. These analyses show how personality and occupation affect perceptions of work conditions. Personality and occupation also affect how workers evaluate work conditions, and personality interacts with worker valuations of work conditions to determine behavior.

Value and Affective Response to Work Conditions

The selectivity observed in internals', externals', and occupation members' perceptions of work conditions is also evident in the way these groups evaluate work conditions. The resources that personality and occupation groups perceive affect reinforcement value, while other *available* resources have no significant effect on reinforcement value. This suggests that workers also evaluate work conditions according to personality and occupational characteristics. These characteristics sensitize group members to particular work conditions while desensitizing them to other work conditions.

Each operative work condition has a cost and a reward dimension. To accurately predict behavioral outcomes, it is important to know how employees evaluate the absolute value (i.e., profit) associated with each work condition. The profit that workers derive from their jobs reflects their perception and valuation of all economic and non-economic job experiences (Thibaut and Kelly, 1959). The analyses in Tables 8 and 15 reveal that these work conditions provide reinforcement cues that are hierarchically ordered within personality and occupational groups. This finding confirms my second hypothesis and suggests further elaboration on the occupation effect on valuations of work conditions. LOC *and* occupation affect the rewards, costs, and profit employees receive from the employment relationship.

Quitting

Each of the exchange relationships examined above provide job costs, job rewards, and profit. Generally, all groups derive costs, rewards, and profit from the same resources. There are, however, significant differences in the magnitude of negative, positive, and absolute reinforcement qualities of the different resources for different groups of workers, and this difference affects their quitting decisions. Personality and occupational groups exhibit an affinity for particular resources. Previous turnover research incorrectly assumed that employee affective responses to work conditions (e.g., job satisfaction) were a function of the same work conditions. This assumption leads one to overlook the subjective availability of resources and to misinterpret their effect on quitting.

Profit is a function of different work conditions for personality and occupational groups. Analyzing quits as a function of work conditions that have universal effects on quitting provides a comparison between workers who receive valuable resources to workers who do not, without understanding the actual workplace dynamics involved in producing value for these employees. The findings above show that this method of predicting behavior is flawed, and that predicting behavior is best achieved by first identifying the reinforcements that motivate different workers.

The review of turnover literature in chapter one examined research that used economic, psychological, and sociological theory to explain turnover. The basic tenets of each theory are incorporated in at least one influential model of turnover. The typical economic model of turnover (see March and Simon, 1958) maintains that economic conditions and human capital variables distribute opportunity among workers. Quitting is the result of rational acts among employees who are trying to maximize profit in the workplace by taking advantage of alternative employment opportunities. Psychological models (see Spector and Michaels, 1986) show that job satisfaction affects quitting and that LOC has a direct effect on this decision. Job satisfaction is a function of worker valuations of work conditions. When job satisfaction is low, internals should quit more than externals. The empirical evidence does not provide conclusive support for this argument. Sociological models (see Price, 1977) also argue that work conditions affect employee job satisfaction, and that alternative job opportunity and job satisfaction affect turnover decisions. These models can be improved by correctly specifying the role of personality.

These analyses show that personality has both direct and indirect effects on quitting. The results in Tables 11, 12, and 17 show how personality indirectly affects quitting. LOC interacts with profit level to determine quitting for all employees in Table 11 and for social counselors in Table 17. The personality × profit interaction effect is demonstrated more strikingly in Table 12. When the sample was divided into internals and externals and analyzed separately, the profit effect on quitting was only significant for internals. The direct effect of LOC appears in the analysis presented in Table 17. Social counselors who have an internal LOC quit more that social counselors who have an external LOC. Understanding how personality affects the valuation of work conditions is necessary for explaining quits. These findings confirmed my fourth hypothesis.

These findings also suggest that economic models that explain quitting as a function of employees' judgment that better alternatives exist would benefit from including personality effects—these interact with their valuations of work conditions. The general theme in research like March and Simon's (1958) suggesting that opportunity is a determinant of quitting behavior is supported by these analyses, but only for eligibility counselors. This model does not explain quits among the other employees in this study.

The social exchange model provides a better explanation of quitting than the economic, psychological, and sociological models reviewed above. Workers tend to quit their jobs when job costs outweigh job rewards and when alternatives are available (Blau, 1964; Emerson, 1981). The analyses in this study confirm this model for internals, social counselors, and employees not differentiated by LOC or occupation.

Mobley (1979), Price (1977), Herzberg, (1974), and March and Simons (1958) have produced important work showing or inferring that work conditions determine turnover. However, they neglected the effect of the interaction between personality and employees' evaluations of work conditions. The evidence presented above shows that this interaction effect is a significant determinant of quitting for the general population of workers, internals, and social counselors. These findings extend current turnover research by specifying the following: first, which work conditions are important to workers in general; second, which work conditions are only important for particular groups of workers; and third, how work conditions and personality interact to determine quitting.

The social exchange model can be applied more generally across employee samples, particularly when employees are not differentiated by personality or occupation. These results suggest, however, that analyzing quits without first understanding personality and occupation effects generates a muddled picture of the turnover process. When data on employee LOC or occupation are available, this information is useful in estimating quitting models that are tailored to specific groups.

Quitting among sub-professionals and other employees who have access to intrinsic work conditions rather than extrinsic work conditions is best analyzed with economic models that consider salary and opportunity variables. Quitting among professionals and other employees who have more extrinsic work conditions that provide greater autonomy, flexibility, and low supervision is explained by the social exchange model. Finally, quitting among employees who have an external LOC should be analyzed with a sociological model such as Price's (1977) that uses demographic variables, work conditions, job satisfaction, and job commitment to explain quitting.

Implications for Future Research

The implications of these findings for turnover research are many. First, a modified social exchange theory proved to be the most effective model for examining quits. Social exchange theory argues that quitting is the outcome of employees' valuation of exchange resources and the availability of alternative sources of profit. Present findings show that personality moderates the effect of profit on quitting, and suggests that the personality effect needs elaboration in the social exchange theory of behavior. Internals and externals and occupation members behaved differently after evaluating the amount of profit they received from their jobs. These interactions should be fully explored in future turnover research. In fact, future behavioral research might benefit by addressing these interactions. This would permit researchers to identify other relationships where the valuation of social and material resources and behavior is moderated by personality. In short, this research strongly supports the modified social exchange model of quitting, and suggests that this modification can be applied to the study of behavior in general.

Second, the findings presented here show that dispositions rather than attitudes are the more useful psychological variables for predicting turnover. Dispositions are more general reflections of personalities than are attitudes. As such, they provide important insight into how workers assess work conditions that is not obtainable when attitudes like job satisfaction are examined. Still, work conditions are likely to contribute to satisfaction and commitment in a hierarchial calculus similar to that which determines job profit.

Price (1977) and Mobley (1982), in particular, and most of the turnover literature consider pay, benefits, supervision, and other work conditions to determine job satisfaction and commitment rather than job profit. Job satisfaction expresses the positive dimension of worker valuations of work conditions. The negative dimension is implied in the absence of job satisfaction. When employed in turnover research, this tendency to view affective responses as having a zero-sum effect on behavior is contrary to findings presented here and elsewhere (Herzberg, 1974; 1985). In contrast, job profit expresses an valuation of positive *and* negative reinforcement qualities of work conditions.

A worker's job satisfaction also depends on his or her expectations and the realization of these expectations. The analysis of quits shows that job satisfaction is more relevant to quit decisions among externals while profit is more relevant for internals. Internals tend to take more responsibility for achieving their goals than externals. Consequently, their expectations may represent a more realistic view of potential outcomes. Externals, on the other hand, may hold more unrealistic or unrealized expectations of outcomes than internals because they believe less in their ability to affect these outcomes. The result of this personalty difference in personal agency is evident in the above findings. Satisfaction is likely to fluctuate most for people who have expectations without the psychological disposition to perceive control over the processes that produce the state. Since externals fit this description more than internals, job satisfaction should be a more important factor for them for predicting behavioral outcomes that are a function of work conditions.

Variation in the LOC and occupational work condition effects on costs and rewards is more significant than variation in the LOC and occupational work condition effects on profit. This suggests that work condition effects on profit are more generalizable. This also underscores the importance of analyzing positive *and* negative evaluations of work conditions. The uni-dimensional positive affect toward work conditions that is reflected in measures of job satisfaction is less important to employees' quit decisions than profit.

Third, in future turnover research, work conditions from the person-organization and person-client exchange relationships should be emphasized. The evaluation of exchange resources in these categories were most important to rewards, costs, and profits received from the employment relationship across employee groups.

Fourth, the findings also show the importance of examining turnover in the context of several workplace relationships. The resources examined in this study derive from person-organization, person-supervisor, person-coworker, and person-client relationships, and resources from each relationship significantly affected worker valuations of the profit they receive from their jobs. However, the March and Simon (1958) model considers only resources exchanged in the person-organization relationship, while the Price model examines resources in each workplace exchange relationship except the person-client relationship. The evidence presented in this study shows that workplace exchange relationships are not equally important to all workers, and that knowing this is important for explaining quitting among different employee groups. More research is needed to determine the resources that best represent each exchange relationship, and if other important relationships exist in the workplace.

Fifth, the manner in which the turnover variable is coded is important for interpreting resource and personality effects on quitting. Coding the dependent variable to contrast quits with stays, transfers, and promotions, as opposed to contrasting quits with stays, significantly affects the logistic regression results. Future research should treat the dichotomous turnover variable with more care by ensuring that the contrast groups are internally homogeneous.

Sixth, job satisfaction reflects employees' attitudes toward work conditions. Profit represents workers' valuations of costs and rewards associated with their work conditions; profit is a characteristic of the job. Future research should compare the uni-dimensional satisfaction affective response to work conditions to models using the rational assessment variable (i.e., profit). This research suggests that using an evaluation that is based on the positive *and* negative reinforcement qualities rather than the positive affective response to work conditions is more useful for explaining quits.

Conclusion

The analyses presented above confirm the importance of considering all relationships in the workplace when attempting to explain affective responses to work conditions, valuations of work conditions, and quitting. The present research shows that exchanges between employees and other actors through the employment relationship affect quitting decisions. Although the person-organization relationship proved to be the most important source of reinforcement for the study sample, other relationships proved to offer resources that affect reinforcement and the quitting decision for some workers. Conventional research practice tends to focus only on person-organization exchanges while ignoring exchanges involving supervisors, coworkers, and clients. Furthermore, the occupations examined here interact with other departments within HSA and with other types of agencies. Exchanges with each of the various organizational and extra-organizational actors may also affect quitting decisions. There is also significant variation in the amount of value employees place on these exchange resources. More research is needed to identify the full range of resources exchanged in the employment relationship, and the types of employees that receive reinforcement from particular resources.

Emerson (1972) argues that organizations are actors in exchange relationships. In addition to supporting Emerson's position, the findings presented above show that employees also maintain exchange relations with supervisors, coworkers, and clients. Accordingly, the evidence overwhelmingly supports the social exchange model of turnover developed in this study. Quitting resulted when the exchange relationships examined produced little profit and when alternatives were available, but only for employees with an internal LOC. Personality interacts with employee valuations of material and social resources to determine quitting. This modified social exchange model predicts quitting for the overall sample, and the subgroups of internals and social counselors.

Quitting among externals and eligibility counselors is determined by different factors. For externals, the sociological model presented by Price (1977) explains quitting as a function of work conditions that determine the level of job satisfaction. For eligibility counselors, the neoclassical economic model presented by March and Simon (1958) that explains turnover as a function of compensation and opportunity for alternative compensation packages appears to explain quits. The implication is that the appropriate model for explaining turnover depends on the diversity of the study population. The improved social exchange model had the broadest application in explaining quits among workers in this sample compared to the other models tested.

Appendix A

INDEPENDENT VARIABLES

Demographic Variables

Tenure in current job (in years)
Region where employed
Marital status
Sex
Age
Race
Occupation
Salary (annual dollars)

Exchange Resources

Case load Size
    I have too much paper work to handle it all effectively?
    My case load is too high to handle it all effectively?
Job autonomy
    How much say do you have over how you do your job?
    How much say do you have over scheduling your job activities?
Routinization
    How many of your work activities are routine?
    How many of your duties are repetitious?
Formal communication
    How well informed does HSA keep you about the following aspects of your job?
        Better methods and techniques to do the job.
        HSA job openings.
        Social events.
        Fringe benefits.
        Agency effectiveness.

Supervisor encouragement
    How true is it that your supervisor...
        is willing to listen your to job-related problems?
        shows you how to improve performance?
        pays attention to what you're saying?
        respects your opinions?
        encourages those (s)he supervises to give their best effort?
Supervisor sex-, race-, age-bias
    How true is it that your supervisor is biased against you...
        because of your sex?
        because of your race or national origin?
        because of your age?
Coworker encouragement
    How true is it that your coworkers...
        are willing to listen to job-related problems?
        show you how to improve performance?
        pay attention to what you're saying?
        respect your opinions?
        encourage each other to give their best effort?
Coworker sex-, race-, age-bias
    How true is it that your coworkers are biased against you...
        because of your sex?
        because of your race or national origin?
        because of your age?
Client deservedness
    Most of my clients are getting a free ride off the taxpayers.
    My clients are lazy.
    My clients are not trying to help themselves.
    My clients are losers.

Exchange Theory

Job rewards
    On a scale of 1 to 9, please circle the number that best indicates to
    what extent there are positive experiences associated with your job.
Job costs
    On a scale of 1 to 9, about what proportion of the time does your
    job involve unpleasant experiences?
Opportunity
    How easy would it be for you to find a job with another employer?

Comparison level
Compared to what I could earn doing similar work for other employers in this area, I believe I am paid:

Personality

Exchange ideology
An employee's work effort should depend partly on how well the organization deals with his or her desires and concerns.
An employee who is treated unfairly should lower his or her work effort.
How hard an employee works should not be affected by how well the organization treats him or her.
An employee's work effort should have nothing to do with fairness of his or her pay.
The failure of this organization to appreciation employee's contribution should not affect how hard he or she works.

LOC

Rotter's (1966) 23 item locus of control scale.

Bibliography

Abdel-Halim, Ahmed H. 1981. "Effects of Role Stress-Job Design-Technology Interaction on Employee Work Satisfaction." *Academy of Management Journal* 24:260–273.

Agho, Augustine O., Charles W. Mueller, and James L. Price. 1993. "Determinants of Employee Job Satisfaction: An Empirical Test of a Causal Model." *Human Relations* 46, No.8:1007–1027.

Allison, Paul D. 1984. *Event History Analysis: Regression for Longitudinal Event Data*. Beverly Hills: Sage.

Allport, Gordon W. 1967. "Attitudes." In *Readings in Attitude Theory and Measurement*, M. Fishbein (ed.), 1–13. New York: Wiley.

Androstane, P. J. and G. Nested. 1976. "Internal-external Control as Contributor to and Outcome of Work Experience." *Journal of Applied Psychology* 61:156–165.

Archer, Robert P. 1979. "Relationships Between Locus of Control, Trait Anxiety, and State Anxiety: An Interaction Perspective." *Journal of Personality* 47:305–316.

Armknecht, Paul, John F. Early. 1972. "Quits in Manufacturing: A Study of Their Causes." *Monthly Labor Review* No. 95 (November): 31–37.

Averitt, Robert. 1968. *The Dual Economy*. New York: Norton.

Bandura, A. 1968. "Social Learning Theory of Identification Processes." In *Handbook of Socialization Theory and Research*, D. Goslin (ed.). Chicago: Rand McNally.

Baron, James, Frank Dobbin and P. Jennings. 1986. "War and Peace: The Industry." *American Journal of Sociology* 92 (September):350–383.

Becker, Gary S. 1975. *Human Capital*. Chicago: The University of Chicago Press.

Beddian, Authur G. and Achilles A. Armenakis. 1981. "A Path-Analytic Study of the Consequences of Role Conflict and Ambiguity." *Academy of Management Journal* 24:417–424.

Berger, S. M. and W. Lambert. 1968. "Stimulus-Response Theory in Contemporary Social Psychology." In The *Handbook of Social Psychology*, G. Lindzey and E. Aronson (eds.), 81–187. New York: Oxford University Press.

Blau, Gary. 1989. "Testing the Generalizability of a Career Commitment Measure and its Impact on Employee Turnover." *Journal of Vocational Behavior* 35 (1):88–103.

Blau, Peter. 1964. *Exchange and Power in Social Life.* New York: John Wiley.

Blegen, Mary A. and Edward J. Lawler. 1989. "Power and Bargaining in Authority-client Relations." *Research in Political Sociology* 4:167–186.

Bluedorn, Allen C. 1982. "The Theories of Turnover: Causes, Effects, and Meaning." *Research in the Sociology of Organizations* 1:75–128.

Braverman, Harry. 1974. *Labor and Monopoly Capital.* Monthly Review.

Buss, David M. and Kenneth H. Craik. 1985. "Why Not Measure That Trait? Alternative Criteria for Identifying Important Dispositions." *Journal of Personality and Social Psychology* 48:934–946.

Carroll, Glenn R. and Karl Ulrich Mayer. 1986. "Job-Shift Patterns in the Federal Republic of Germany: The Effects of Social Class, Industrial Sector, and Organizational Size." *American Sociological Review* 51 (June):323–341.

Carsten, Jeanne M. and Paul E. Spector. 1987. "Unemployment, Job Satisfaction, and Employee Turnover: A Meta-analytic Test of the Muchinsky Model." *Journal of Applied Psychology* 72 (3):374–381.

Chein, I. 1967. "Behavior Theory and the Behavior of Attitudes: Some Critical Comments." In *Readings in Attitude Theory and Measurement.* M. Fishbein (ed.), 51–57. New York: Wiley.

Colarelli, Stephen M., Roger A. Dean, and Constantine Konstans. 1987. "Comparative Effects of Personal and Situational Influences on Job Outcomes of New Professionals." *Journal of Applied Psychology* 72 (4):558–566.

Collier, P., J. B. Knight. 1986. "Wage Structure and Labour Turnover." *Oxford Economic Paper* 38:77–93.

Cook, K. 1975. "Expectations, Evaluations, and Equity." *American Sociological Review* 40:372–388.

Cornfield, Daniel B. 1985. "Economic Segmentation and Expression of Labor Unrest." *Social Science Quarterly* 66 (2):248–265.

———. 1987. "Workers, Managers, and Technological Change." In *Workers, Managers, and Technological Change.* D. Cornfield (ed.), 3–24. New York: Plenum Press.

Cotton, John L. and Jeffrey M. Tuttle. 1986. "Employee Turnover: A Meta-analysis and Review with Implications for Research." *Academy of Management Review* 11 (1):55–70.

Dalton, Dan R., William D. Todor. 1979. "Turnover Turned Over: An Expanded and Positive Perspective." *Academy of Management Review* 4, No. 2:225–235.

Dewar, Robert, and James Werbel. 1979. "Universalistic and Contingency Predictions of Employee Satisfaction and Conflict." *Administrative Science Quarterly* 24:426–446.

DiPrete, Thomas A. 1987. "Horizontal and Vertical Mobility in Organizations." *Administrative Science Quarterly* 32:422–44.

Distefano Jr., M. K., Margaret W. Pryer. 1982. "Ability, Training Performance, and Demographic Factors in Voluntary Turnover Among Psychiatric Aides." *Psychological Reports* 51:619–622, 1982.

Doeringer, Peter and Michael J. Piore. 1971. *Internal Labor Markets and Manpower Analysis*. Lexington, MA: Heath.

Doob, L. W. 1967. "The Behavior of Attitudes." In *Readings in Attitude Theory and Measurement*, M. Fishbein (ed.), 42–50. New York: Wiley.

Dougherty, Thomas W., Allen C. Bluedorn, and Thomas L. Keon. 1985. "Precursors of Employee Turnover: A Multiple-sample Causal Analysis." *Journal of Occupational Behavior* 6:259–271.

Eisenberger, Robert, Robin Huntington, Steven Hutchison, and Debora Sowa. 1986. "Perceived Organizational Support." *Journal of Applied Psychology* 71 (3):500–507.

Elder, Jr. Glen H. 1973. "On Linking Social Structure and Personality." *American Behavior Scientist* 16 (6):785–800.

Emerson, Richard M. 1962. "Power-Dependent Relations." *American Sociological Review* 27:31–40.

———. 1972. "Exchange Theory, Part 2: Exchange Relations and Network Structure." In *Sociological Theories in Progress*, J. Berger, M. Zelditch and B. Anderson (eds.), 38–87. New York: Houghton Mifflin.

———. 1981. "Social Exchange Theory." In *Social Psychology*, Morris Rosenberg and Ralph Turner, (eds.), 30–64. New York: Basic Books.

Endler, N. S. and D. Magnusson. 1976. *Interactional Psychology and Personality*. New York: Wiley.

Farrell, Daniel and Caryl E. Rusbult. 1981. "Exchange Variables as Predictors of Job Satisfaction, Job Commitment, and Turnover: The Impact of Rewards, Costs, Alternatives, and Investments." *Organizational Behavior and Human Performance* 27 (28):78–95.

———. 1992. "Exploring the Exit, Voice, Loyalty, and Neglect Typology: The Influence of Job Satisfaction, Quality of Alternatives, and Investment Size." *Employee Responsibilities and Rights Journal* 5, No. 3:201–218, 1992.

Farris, Gerald R., Stuart A. Youngblood, and Valerie L Yates. 1985. "Personality, Training Performance, and Withdrawal: A Test of the Person-Group fit Hypothesis for Organizational Newcomers." *Journal of Vocational Behavior* 27 (3):377–388.

Fishbein, M. 1967. "Attitude and the Prediction of Behavior." In *Readings in Attitude Theory and Measurement*, M. Fishbein (ed.), 477– 492. New York: Wiley.

Fishbein, M. and I. Ajzen. 1975. *Belief, Attitude, Intention and Behavior: An Introduction to Theory and Research*. Reading, MA: Addison-Wesley.

Freud, Sigmund. 1962. *Civilization and Its Discontents*. New York: Dorsey Press.

Furnham, Adrian and Rosemary Schaeffer. 1984. "Person-Environment Fit, Job Satisfaction and Mental Health." *Journal of Occupational Psychology* 57:295–307.

Ganster, Daniel C. and Marcelline R. Fusilier. 1989. "Control in the Workplace." *International Review of Industrial and Organizational Psychology*, eds, C.I. Cooper and I. Robertson, John Wiley and Sons Ltd.

Gerhart, Barry. 1987. "How Important are Dispositional Factors as Determinants of Job Satisfaction? Implications for Job Design and other Personnel Programs." *Journal of Applied Psychology* 72 (3):366–373.

Glisson, Charles, Mark Durick. 1988. "Predictors of Job Satisfaction and Organizational Commitment in Human Service Organizations." *Administrative Quarterly* 33:61–81.

Goffman, E. 1959. *The Presentation of Self in Everyday Life*. Garden City, New York: Doubleday.

Goodman, Sherri H. and L.K. Waters. 1987. "Convergent Validity of Five Locus of Control Scales." *Education and Psychological Measurement* 47:743–47.

Gottfredson, L. 1978. "An Analytical Description of Employment According to Race, Sex, Prestige and Holland Type of Work." *Journal of Vocational Behavior* 13:210–221.

Gove, W. and M. Geerken. 1977. "The Effect of Children and Employment on the Mental Health of Married Men and Women." *Social Forces* 56,1 (September):66–76.

Graham, Jill W, and Michael Keeley. "Hirschman's Loyalty Construct." *Employee Responsibilities and Rights Journal* 5, No. 3:191–200, 1992.

Granovetter, Mark. 1986. "Labor Mobility, Internal Markets, and Job Matching: A Comparison of the Sociological and Economic Approaches." *Research in Social Stratification and Mobility* 5:3–39.
———. 1973. "The Strength of Weak Ties." *American Journal of Sociology* 78 (6):1360–1380.
Greenhalgh, Leonard. 1980. "A Process Model of Organizational Turnover: The Relationship With Job Security as a Case in Point." *Academy of Management Review* 5, No. 2, 299–303.
Griffeth, Rodger W. and Peter W. Hom. 1988. "Locus of Control and Delay of Gratification as Moderators of Employee Turnover." *Journal of Applied Social Psychology* 18 (15, pt1) 1318–1333.
Halaby, Charles N and David L. Weakliem. 1989. "Worker Control and Attachment to the Firm." *American Journal of Sociology* 95:3:549–491.
———. 1988. "Action and Information in the Job Mobility Process: The Search Decision." *American Sociological Review* 53:1:9–15.
Hall, C. S. and G. Lindzey. 1970. "Stimulus Response Theory" and "Skinner's Operant Reinforcement Theory." In *Theories of Personality,* 417–514. 2nd Edition. New York: John Wiley.
Haynes, Karen. 1979. "Job Satisfaction of Mid-management Social Workers." *Administration in Social Work* 3:207–217.
Heath, Anthony. 1976. *Rational Choice and Social Exchange.* Cambridge: Cambridge University.
Hegtvedt, Karen A. 1988. "Social Determinants of Perception: Power, Equity, and Status Effects in an Exchange Situation." *Social Psychology Quarterly* 51 (2):141–153.
Herzberg, Frederick. 1974. "Motivation-Hygiene Profiles: Pinpointing what Ails the Organization." Organizational Dynamics 3 (2):18–29.
Hill, Richard. 1981. "Attitudes and Behavior." In *Social Psychology: Sociology Perspectives*, Morris Rosenberg and Ralph Turner (eds.), 347–377. New York: Basic.
Hodson, Randy and Teresa A. Sullivan. 1985. "Totem or Tyrant? Monopoly, Regional, and Local Sector Effects on Worker Commitment." *Social Forces* 63 (3):716–731.
Hom, P. W., R. Katerberg, and C.L. Hulin. 1979. "Comparative Examination of Three Approaches to the Prediction of Turnover." *Journal of Applied Psychology* 64:280–290.
Homans, G. C. 1974. *Social Behavior: Its Elementary Forms*, 2nd edition. New York: Harcourt, Brace and World.

Howell, Frank and William Reese. 1986. "Sex and Mobility in the Dual Economy: From Entry to Mid-career." *Work and Occupations* 13 (February):77–96.

Hui, Harry C. 1988. "Impacts of Objective and Subjective Labour Market Conditions on Employee Turnover." *Journal of Occupational Psychology* 61 (3):211–219.

Ippolito, Richard A. 1987. "Why Federal Workers Don't Quit." *The Journal of Human Resources* 22, No. 2:381–399.

Jackofshy, Ellen F., Lawrence H. Peters. 1983. "Job Turnover Versus Company Turnover: Reassessment of the March and Simon Participation Hypothesis." *Journal of Applied Psychology* 68 (3):490–495.

Kalleberg, Arne L. 1989. "Linking Macro and Micro Levels: Bringing the Workers Back into the Sociology of Work." *Social Forces* 67 (3):582–592.

Katz, Ralph. 1978. "Job Longevity as a Situational Factor in Job Satisfaction." *Administrative Science Quarterly* 23:204–223.

Kirton, M. J. and R. M. McCarthy. 1988. "Cognitive Climate and Organizations." *Journal of Occupational Psychology* 61:175–184.

Knapp, Martin, Kostas Harissis, and Spyros Missiakoulis. 1981. "Who Leaves Social Work?" *British Journal of Social Work* 11:421–444.

Koch, James L. and Richard M. Steers. 1978. "Job Attachment, Satisfaction, and Turnover Among Public Sector Employees." *Journal of Vocational Behavior* 12 (1):119–128.

Kohn, Melvin. 1981. "Personality, Occupation, and Social Stratification: a Frame of Reference." *Research in Social Stratification and Mobility*, 1:267–297.

———. 1982. "Occupational Structure and Alienation." *American Journal of Sociology* 82 (1):111–130.

———. 1989. "Social Structure and Personality: A Quintessentially Sociological Approach to Social Psychology." *Social Forces* 69 (1):26–33.

Kotelock, Peter, Philip Blumstein, and Pepper Schwartz. 1976. *Prognosis Negative: Crisis in the Health Care System.* New York: Vintage Books.

Krackhardt, David, Lyman W. Porter. 1985. "When Friends Leave: A Structural Analysis of the Relationship Between Turnover and Stayers' Attitudes." *Administrative Science Quarterly* 30:242–261.

Krecker, Margeret L. "Work Careers and Organizational Careers: The Effects of Age and Tenure on Worker Attachment to the Employment Relationship." *Work and Occupations* 21, No. 3:251–283, 1994.

―――. 1986. "The Snowball Effect: Turnover Embedded in Communication Networks." *Journal of Applied Psychology* 7 No. 1:50–55.

Krueger, A. and L. H. Summers. 1987. "Reflections on the Inter-industry Wage Structure." In *Unemployment and the Structure of Labor Markets,* K. Lang and J. Leonard (eds.). Oxford: Blackwell.

Lamphere, Louise. 1985. "Bringing the Family to Work: Women's Culture on the Shop Floor." *Feminist Studies* 11 (Fall):519–540.

LaPiere, R. T. 1967. "Attitudes Versus Actions." In *Readings in Attitude Theory and Measurement,* M. Fishbein (ed.), 14–25. New York: Wiley.

Lefcourt, Herbert M. 1982. *Locus of Control: Current Trends in Theory and Research.* New Jersey: Lawrence Erlbaum Associates, Inc.

Leonard, Jonathan S. 1987. "Carrots and Sticks: Pay, Supervision, and Turnover." *Journal of Labor Economics* 5, No. 4:S136–S152.

Lock, E. A. 1976. "The Nature and Causes of Job Satisfaction." In *Handbook of Industrial and Organizational Psychology,* M.D. Dunnette (ed.). Chicago: Rand McNally.

Lott, Bernice E. 1967. "Attitude Formation: The Development of a Color-Preference Response Through Mediated Generalization." In *Readings in Attitudes Theory and Measurement,* M. Fishbein (ed.), 366–372. New York: Wiley.

Lott, Bernice and Albert J. Lott. 1985. "Learning Theory in Contemporary Social Psychology." *The Handbook of Social Psychology* 1:109–136.

Lumpkin, James R. 1985. "Validity of a Brief Locus of Control Scales for Survey Research." *Psychological Reports* 57:655–59.

March, J. G. and H. A. Simons. 1958. *Organizations.* New York: Wiley.

Marx, Karl. 1977 (1967). *Capital.* Volume 1. New York: International Publishers.

McEvoy, Glenn M. and Wayne F. Cascio. 1985. "Strategies for Reducing Employee Turnover: A Meta-Analysis." *Journal of Applied Psychology* 70 (2):342–353.

Mirels, Herbert L. 1970. "Dimensions of Internal Versus External Control." *Journal of Consulting and Clinical Psychology* 34 (2):226–28.

Mobley, William H. 1982. *Employee Turnover: Causes, Consequences, and Control.* Reading: Addison-Wesley Publishing Co.

Mobley, W. H., R. W. Griffeth, H. H. Hand, B. M. Meglino. 1979. "Review and Conceptual Analysis of the Employee Turnover Process." *Psychological Bulletin* 86, No. 3, 493–522.

Molm, Linda D. 1989. "Punishment Power: A Balancing Process in Power-Dependent Relations." *American Journal of Sociology* 94 (6):1392–1418.

Moos, Rudolf H. 1986. "Work as a Human Context." In *Psychology and Work*, M. Pallak and R. Perloff (eds.). Washington, D.C.: American Psychological Association.

Mowday, R. T. and D. G. Spencer. 1981. "The Influence of Task and Personality Characteristics on Employee Turnover and Absenteeism Incidents." *Academy of Management Journal* 24:634–642.

Mowday, R. T., L. W. Porter, and R. M. Steers. *Employee-organization Linkages*. New York: Academic Press. 1982.

Mowday, R. T., R. M. Steers, and L. W. Porter. 1979. "The Measurement of Organizational Commitment." *Journal of Vocational Behavior* 14:224–227.

Muchinsky, Paul M. and M. L. Tuttle. 1979. "Employee Turnover: An Empirical and Methodological Assessment." *Journal of Vocational Behavior* 14:43–77.

Muchinsky, Paul M. and Paula C. Morrow. 1980. "A Multidisciplinary Model of Voluntary Employee Turnover." *Journal of Human Behavior* 17, 263–290.

Mueller, Charles W., E. Marcia Boyer, and James L. Price. "Employee Attachment and Noncoercive Conditions of Work: The Case of Dental Hygienists." *Work and Occupations* 21, No. 2:179–212. 1994.

Mueller, Charles W., Jean E. Wallace, and James L. Price. "Employee Commitment: Resolving Some Issues." *Work and Occupations* 19, No. 3:211–236, 1992.

O'Brien, G. E. 1984. "Locus of Control, Work, and Retirement." In *Research in the Locus of Control*, H. M. Lefcourt (ed.), Vol 3:7–72. New York: Academic Press.

O'Connor, Edward, Lawrence Peters, Abdullah Pooyan, Jeff Weekly, Blake Frank, and Bruce Erenkrantz. 1984. "Situational Constraint Effects on Performance, Affective Reactions, and Turnover: A Field Replication and Extension." *Journal of Applied Psychology* 69 (4):663–672.

O'Reilly, C.A. III, and D.F. Caldwell. 1981. "The Commitment and Job Tenure of New Employees: Some Evidence of Post-decisional Justification." *Administrative Science Quarterly* 19:357–365.

O'Reilly III, Charles, David Caldwell, and William Barnett. 1989. "Work Group Demography, Social Integration, and Turnover." *Administrative Science Quarterly* 34:21–37.

O'Reilly III, Charles and Jennifer Chatman. 1986. "Organizational Commitment and Psychological Attachment: The Effects of Compliance, Identification, and Internalization on Prosocial Behavior." *Journal of Applied Psychology* 71 (3):492–499.

Orpen, Christopher. 1986. "The Effect of Job Performance on the Relationship Between Job Satisfaction and Turnover." *The Journal of Social Psychology* 126 (2):277–278.

Perloff, Stephen H. 1971. "Comparing Municipal Salaries With Industry and Federal Pay." *Monthly Labor Review* October:46–50.

Phares, E. J. 1973. *Locus of Control: A Personality Determinant of Behavior*. Morristown, N.J.: General Learning Press.

Piore, Michael J. 1972. "Notes for a Theory of Labor Market Stratification." From Dan Dalton and William Todor. "Turnover Turned Over: An Expanded and Positive Perspective." *Academy of Management Review* 4 (2):225–235. 1979.

Price, James. 1977. *The Study of Turnover*. Ames: Iowa State University Press.

Price, James, and C. W. Mueller. 1981. *The Study of Turnover*. New York: SP Medical and Scientific Books.

Rhine, R.J. 1967. "A Concept Formation Approach to Attitude Acquisition." In *Readings in Attitude Theory and Measurement*, M. Fishbein (ed.), 382–388. New York: Wiley.

Ritzer, George. 1989. "Sociology of Work: A Metatheoretical Analysis." *Social Forces* 67 (3):593–604.

Ronen, Simcha and Simcha Sadan. 1984. "Job Attitudes Among Different Occupational Status Groups." *Work and Occupations* 11 (1):77–97.

Rosenberg, M. J. 1967. "Cognitive Structure and Attitudinal Affect." In *Readings in Attitude Theory And Measurement*, M. Fishbein (ed.), 325–331. New York: Wiley.

Rotter, Julian B. 1966. "Generalized Expectancies for Internal Versus External Control of Reinforcement." *Psychological Monographs: General and Applied* 80 (1):1–28.

Rusbult, Caryl E. 1980. "Commitment and Satisfaction in Romantic Associations: A Test of the Investment Model." *Journal of Experimental Social Psychology* 16:172–186.

Rusbult, Caryl E., Dan Farrell. 1983. "A Longitudinal Test of the Investment Model: The Impact on Job Satisfaction, Job Commitment, and Turnover of Variations in Rewards, Costs, Alternatives, and Investments." *Journal of Applied Psychology* 68 (3):429–438.

Saunders, David M., Blair H. Sheppard, Virginia Knight, and Jonelle Roth. 1992. "Employee Voice to Supervisors." *Employee Responsibilities and Rights Journal* 5, No. 3:241–259.

Schoenherr, R. A. and A. M. Greeley. 1974. "Role Commitment Processes and the American Catholic Priesthood." *American Sociological Review* 39:407–426.

Shaw, Barry M. and Philip Costanzo. 1970. *Theories of Social Psychology.* New York: McGraw Hill.

Shorey, John. 1983. "An Analysis of Sex Differences in Quits." Oxford Economic Papers 35 (2):213–22.

Simpson, Ida H. 1989. "The Sociology of Work: Where Have the Workers Gone?" *Social Forces* 67 (3):563–581.

Sims, H. P., A. D. Szilagyi, and R. T. Keller. 1976. "The Measurement of Job Characteristics." *Academy of Management Journal* 19:195–212.

Singer, Eleanor. 1981. "Reference Groups and Social Evaluations."In *Social Psychology,* Morris Rosenberg and Ralph H. Turner (eds.), 66–93. New York: Basic Books.

Smith, Adam. 1965 (1776). *The Wealth of Nations.* New York: Modern Library.

Smith, M. B. 1967. "The Personal Setting of Public Opinion: A Study of Attitudes Toward Russia." In *Readings in Attitudes Theory and Measurement,* M. Fishbein (ed.), 58–70. New York: Wiley.

Snyder, Mark and William Ickes. 1985. "Personality and Social Behavior." *The Handbook of Social Psychology* 2: 880–940.

Spector, Paul E. 1982. "Behavior in Organizations as a Function of Employee's Locus of Control." *Psychological Bulletin* 91 (3):482–497.

_____. 1985. "Measurement of Human Service Staff Satisfaction: Development of the Job Satisfaction Survey." *American Journal of Community Psychology* 13 (6):693–713.

Spector, Paul E., Charles E. Michaels. 1986. "Personality and Employee Withdrawal: Effect of Locus of Control on Turnover." *Psychological Reports* 59:63–66.

Staats, A. W. 1967. "An Outline of an Integrated Learning Theory of Attitude Formation and Function." In *Readings in Attitude Theory and Measurement,* M. Fishbein (ed.), 373–376. New York: Wiley.

Staats, A. W. and C. K. Staats. 1967. "Attitudes Established by Classical Conditioning." In *Readings in Attitude Theory and Measurement*, M. Fishbein (ed.), 377-381. New York: Wiley.

Staine, G. L., K. J. Pottik and D. A. Fudge. 1986. "Wives' Employment and Husbands' Attitudes Towards Work and Life." *Journal of Applied Psychology* 71:118-128.

Staw, Barry M. and Jerry Ross. 1985. "Stability in the Midst of Change: A Dispositional Approach to Job Attitudes." *Journal of Applied Psychology* 70 (3):469-480.

Staw, Barry M., Nancey E. Bell, and John A. Clausen. 1986. "The Dispositional Approach to Job Attitudes: A Lifetime Longitudinal Test." *Administrative Science Quarterly* 31:56-77.

Steel, Robert P., Nestor K. Ovalle, 2d. 1984. "A Review and Meta-Analysis of Research on the Relationship Between Behavioral Intentions and Employee Turnover." *Journal of Applied Psychology* Vol. 69, No. 4:673-686.

Stinchcombe, A. L. 1979. "Social Mobility in Industrial Labor Markets." *Acta Sociologica* 22:217-245.

Swafford, Michael. 1980. "Three Parametric Techniques For Contingency Table Analysis: A Nontechnical Commentary." *American Sociological Review* 45:664-690.

Thibaut, J. W. and H. H. Kelley. 1959. *The Social Psychology of Groups*. New York: Wiley.

Thomas, W. I. 1978. "The Definition of the Situation." In *Symbolic Interaction: A Reader In Psychology*, 3rd. Edition, J. Manis and B. Meltzer (eds.), 254-258. Boston: Allyn and Bacon, Inc.

Thompson, Kenneth R., Willbann D. Terpening. 1983."Job-type Variations and Antecedents to Intention to Leave: A Content Approach to Turnover." *Human Relations* 36, No. 7:655-682.

Tiffany, Paula R. 1986. "The Impact of Behavioral Intentions on Voluntary and Involuntary Turnover: A Test of Significance." *Unpublished Dissertation* No. 543, Peabody College.

Todor, Willian D., Dan R. Dalton. 1986. "Workers Stay Longer When They Have a Chance to Transfer." *Sociology and Social Research* 70 (4):276.

Totman, R. 1973. "An Approach to Cognitive Dissonance: Case Study of Evolution of a Theory." *Psychological Review* 85:53-57.

Tziner, Sharon E. and Yoav Vardi. 1984. "Work Satisfaction and Absenteeism Among Social Workers: The Role of Altruistic Values." *Work and Occupations* 11 (4):461-470.

U.S. Department of Labor Bureau of Labor Statistics. 1980. "Employment and Unemployment During 1979: An Analysis." *Special Labor Force Report*, 234. Washington, D.C. 20212.

Utgoff, Kathleen C. 1983. "Compensation Levels and Quit Rates in the Public Sector." *The Journal of Human Resources* 18 (3):394–406.

Verdieck, Mary J., Joseph J. Shields, and Dean R. Hoge. 1988. "Role Commitment Processes Revisited: American Catholic Priests 1970 and 1985." *Journal for the Scientific Study of Religion* 27 (4):524–535.

Villemez, Wayne J. and William P. Bridges. 1988. "When Bigger is Better: Differences in the Individual-Level Effect of Firm and Establishment Size." *American Sociological Review* 53 (April): 237–255.

Waters, L. K., Darrell Roach, Carrie W. Waters. 1976. "Estimates of Future Tenure, Satisfaction, and Biographical Variables as Predictors of Termination." *Personnel Psychology* 29:57–60.

Wegener, Bernard. 1991. "Job Mobility and Social Ties: Social Resources, Prior Job, and Status Attainment." *American Sociological Review* 1 (February):60-70.

Weisberg, Jacob and Alan Kirschenbaum. "Gender and Turnover: A Re-examination of the Impact of Sex on Intent and Actual Job Changes." *Human Relations* 46, No. 8:987–1007, 1993.

Werbel, James D., Sam Gould. 1984. "A Comparison of the Relationship of Commitment to Turnover in Recent Hires and Tenured Employees." *Journal of Applied Psychology* 69. No. 4:687–690.

Wiggings, J., D. Lederer, A. Salkowe, and G. Rys. 1983. "Job Satisfaction Related to Tested Congruence and Differentiation." *Journal of Vocational Behavior* 23:112–121.

Youngblood, Stuart A., William H. Mobley, Bruce M. Meglino. 1983. "A Longitudinal Analysis of the Turnover Process." *Journal of Applied Psychology* 68, No. 3:507–516.

Index

Age, 26, 27, 31, 33, 34, 40-43, 45, 48, 54-59, 61, 67, 68, 77, 78, 93, 94
Allport, Gordon, 4
Analyses, 20, 23, 25, 31, 33, 35, 36, 39, 42, 43, 46, 51, 53-55, 58-60, 63, 66, 69, 70, 73, 75-77, 79, 80, 82-87, 89, 90
  Regression, 31, 34-36, 9, 43, 45-48, 51, 53-57, 59, 61, 66, 68, 70, 74, 76-78, 83, 90
  T-tests, 39, 40, 66, 67, 74
Archer, Robert, 14
Armknecht, Paul, 5, 6, 8
Averitt, Robert, 6

Becker, Gary, 7, 8

Chein, I., 10
Clients, interaction with, 9, 20, 28, 39, 40, 42, 45, 46, 48, 52, 54, 56-59, 61, 64, 66-69, 70, 72, 73, 75, 78-80, 82, 83, 90, 91, 94
Commitment, 10-17, 19, 26, 27, 29, 41, 56, 57, 61, 78, 88, 89
Comparison level, 26, 30, 39, 41, 54, 58, 59, 94
Cornfield, Daniel, 4, 6
Coworkers, 20-22, 26, 27, 39-42, 45, 46, 48, 65, 73, 75, 79, 82, 83, 90, 91, 94
  bias, 27, 53, 54, 56, 57, 61, 78, 94

encouragement, 27, 41, 45, 48, 53, 61, 67, 68, 73, 75, 94

Dalton, Dan, 6, 24
Dependent variable, 24, 31, 35, 55, 59, 90
Disability claims examiners, 23, 31, 34, 35, 55, 56, 57, 61, 64-70, 75, 76, 79, 82
Doob, L.W., 10
Dual Labor Market, 5-8

Eligibility counselors, 23, 31, 32, 34, 55, 56, 57, 61, 64-70, 72-77, 79, 80, 82, 83, 87, 91
Emerson, Richard, 17, 18, 20, 22, 87, 91
Exchange ideology, 22, 23, 25, 26, 39, 42, 43, 45, 46, 53, 55-57, 59, 61, 77, 78, 95
Exchange resources, 4, 13, 16-22, 26, 27, 35, 39-43, 45-48, 51-54, 58-60, 63, 65-70, 72-76, 79-82, 84-86, 88-91, 93
Exchange theory, 4, 17-20, 22, 29, 30, 43, 88, 94

Farrell, Daniel, 8, 10, 17, 19, 23, 27, 29, 30
Fishbein, M., 4, 9-11, 47
Formal communication, 26-28, 40, 41, 43, 45, 48, 51-53, 55, 61, 64, 66-69, 72-74, 78, 79, 83, 93

Coding, 24, 59, 90

Utgoff, Kathleen, 5, 6
Utility Maximization Theory, 5,
   8

Value, in the workplace, 4, 9,
   12, 13, 17-19, 21, 22, 30,
   39, 40, 47, 52, 53, 63, 70,
   72-75, 79, 85, 86, 91

Vocational   Rehabilitation
   Counselors, 23, 33-35, 56, 57,
   61, 64-70, 72-76, 79, 82

Work Conditions, 3, 4, 6, 7, 9,
   10, 13-16, 18-21, 25, 26,
   33, 39, 42, 43, 46, 54, 55,
   58-60, 63-66, 70, 73,
   75-77, 80-91